PS595.   68-3462
H5   Vincent
V5   Patriotic poems America
Pa   loves
1968

Date Due

JUL   2000

OCT 9 '69		JUN 2004
		JUN 09
		JUL X X 2015

PRINTED IN U.S.A.

PATRIOTIC POEMS AMERICA LOVES

PATRIOTIC POEMS
AMERICA LOVES

125 poems commemorating stirring
historical events and American ideals

Compiled by Jean Anne Vincent

ILLUSTRATED BY RAY CRUZ

DOUBLEDAY & COMPANY, INC.
GARDEN CITY, NEW YORK
1968

Design by Jeanette Portelli

Grateful acknowledgment is made to the following for the use of material under their control:

Abingdon Press, for "The Name of Washington" by Arthur Gordon Field, from *Poems for the Great Days* compiled by Thomas Curtis Clark and Robert L. Clark. Copyright 1948 by Stone and Pierce (Abingdon Press). Used by permission.

Anderson House, for "Lafayette to Washington" from *Valley Forge* by Maxwell Anderson. Copyright 1934 by Maxwell Anderson, copyright renewed 1962 by Gilda Anderson, Alan Anderson, Terence Anderson, Quentin Anderson, and Hesper A. Levenstein. All rights reserved. Used by permission.

A. S. Barnes & Company, Inc., for "The First Division Marches" by Grantland Rice. Used by permission.

The Bobbs-Merrill Company, Inc., for "One Country" from *Comes One with a Song* by Frank L. Stanton. Used by permission.

Brandt & Brandt, for "John Adams" from *A Book of Americans* by Rosemary and Stephen Vincent Benét (Holt, Rinehart and Winston, Inc.), copyright 1933 by Rosemary and Stephen Vincent Benét, copyright renewed © 1961 by Rosemary Carr Benét; for "American Muse" (from *John Brown's Body*) by Stephen Vincent Benét from *The Selected Works of Stephen Vincent Benét* (Holt, Rinehart and Winston, Inc.), copyright 1927, 1928 by Stephen Vincent Benét, copyright renewed © 1955 by Rosemary Carr Benét; and for "Written in a Time of Crisis" (from

Billy Rose Enterprises, for "The Unknown Soldier" by Billy Rose. Used by permission.

The Ben Roth Agency, Inc., for "In Flanders Fields" by John McCrae. Copyright © Punch Publications, Ltd. Used by permission.

Charles Scribner's Sons, for "America for Me" from *The Poems of Henry van Dyke;* and for "Lexington" from *Poems* by Sidney Lanier. Used by permission.

Shapiro, Bernstein & Co., Inc., for "The Caisson Song" by Edmund L. Gruber. Used by permission.

The Society of Authors and Dr. John Masefield, O.M., for "John Fitzgerald Kennedy" by John Masefield. Used by permission.

Nancy Byrd Turner, for her poem "The First Thanksgiving of All." Used by permission.

A. Watkins, Inc., for "Atlantic Charter: 1942" by Francis Brett Young. Copyright © 1944 by Francis Brett Young. Used by permission.

PATRIOTIC POEMS AMERICA LOVES

AMERICA

Samuel Francis Smith

My country, 'tis of thee,
Sweet land of liberty,
    Of thee I sing;
Land where my fathers died,
Land of the pilgrims' pride,
From every mountain-side
    Let Freedom ring.

My native country, thee,
Land of the noble free,—
    Thy name I love;

I love thy rocks and rills,
Thy woods and templed hills;
My heart with rapture thrills
    Like that above.

Let music swell the breeze,
And ring from all the trees
    Sweet Freedom's song;
Let mortal tongues awake,
Let all that breathe partake,
Let rocks their silence break,
    The sound prolong.

Our fathers' God, to Thee,
Author of liberty,
    To Thee we sing;
Long may our land be bright
With Freedom's holy light;
Protect us by Thy might,
    Great God, our King.

A NATIONAL HYMN

from *Miss Ravenel's Conversion*

John William DeForest

Be thou our country's Chief
In this our age of grief,
    Allfather great;
Go forth with awful tread,
Crush treason's serpent head,
Bring back our sons misled,
    And save our State.

Uphold our stripes and stars
Through war's destroying jars
    With thy right hand;
O God of battles, lead
Where our swift navies speed,
Where our brave armies bleed
    For fatherland.

Break every yoke and chain,
Let truth and justice reign
    From sea to sea;
Make all our statutes right
In thy most holy sight;
Light us, O Lord of light,
    To follow Thee.

God bless our fatherland,
God make it strong and grand
    On sea and shore;
Ages its glory swell,
Peace in its borders dwell,
God stand its sentinel
    For evermore.

AMERICA

Arlo Bates

For, O America, our country!—land
  Hid in the west through centuries, till men
Through countless tyrannies could understand
  The priceless worth of freedom,—once again
The world was new-created when thy shore
  First knew the Pilgrim keels, the one last test
The race might make of manhood, nor give o'er
  The strife with evil till it proved its best.
Thy true sons stand as torch-bearers, to hold
  A guiding light. Here the last stand is made.
If we fail here, what new Columbus bold,
  Steering brave prow through black seas unafraid,
Finds out a fresh land where man may abide
  And freedom yet be saved? The whole round earth
Has seen the battle fought. Where shall men hide
  From tyranny and wrong, where life have worth,
If here the cause succumb? If greed of gold
  Or lust of power or falsehood triumph here,
The race is lost! A globe dispeopled, cold,
  Rolled down the void a voiceless, lifeless sphere,
Were not so stamped by all which hope debars
  As were this earth, plunging along through space
Conquered by evil, shamed among the stars,
  Bearing a base, enslaved, dishonored race!
Here has the battle its last vantage ground;
  Here all is won, or here must all be lost;
Here freedom's trumpets one last rally sound;

Here to the breeze its blood-stained flag is tossed.
America, last hope of man and truth,
    The name must through all coming ages be
The badge unspeakable of shame and ruth,
    Or glorious pledge that man through truth is free.
This is thy destiny; the choice is thine
    To lead all nations and outshine them all;—
But if thou failest, deeper shame is thine,
    And none shall spare to mock thee in thy fall.

AMERICA

Sydney Dobell

Nor force nor fraud shall sunder us! Oh ye
Who north or south, on east or western land,
Native to noble sounds, say truth for truth,
Freedom for freedom, love for love, and God
For God; oh ye who in eternal youth
Speak with a living and creative flood
This universal English, and do stand
Its breathing book; live worthy of that grand
Heroic utterance—parted, yet a whole,
Far, yet unsevered—children brave and free
Of the great Mother-tongue, and ye shall be
Lords of an empire wide as Shakespeare's soul,
Sublime as Milton's immemorial theme,
And rich as Chaucer's speech, and fair as Spenser's dream.

OUR COUNTRY

Julia Ward Howe

On primal rocks she wrote her name;
  Her towers were reared on holy graves;
The golden seed that bore her came
  Swift-winged with prayer on ocean waves.

The Forest bowed his solemn crest,
  And open flung his sylvan doors;
Meek Rivers led the appointed guest
  To clasp the wide-embracing shores;

Till, fold by fold, the broidered land
  To swell her virgin vestments grew,
While sages, strong in heart and hand,
  Her virtue's fiery girdle drew.

O exile of the wrath of kings!
  O Pilgrim Ark of Liberty!
The refuge of divinest things,
  Their record must abide in thee!

First in the glories of thy front
  Let the crown-jewel, Truth, be found;
Thy right hand fling, with generous wont,
  Love's happy chain to farthest bound!

Let Justice, with the faultless scales,
  Hold fast the worship of thy sons;
Thy Commerce spread her shining sails
  Where no dark tide of rapine runs!

So link thy ways to those of God,
  So follow firm the heavenly laws,
That stars may greet thee, warrior-browed,
  And storm-sped angels hail thy cause!

O Lord, the measure of our prayers,
  Hope of the world in grief and wrong,
Be thine the tribute of the years,
  The gift of Faith, the crown of Song!

ONE COUNTRY

Frank L. Stanton

After all,
One country, brethren! We must rise or fall
With the Supreme Republic. We must be
The makers of her immortality;
  Her freedom, fame,
  Her glory or her shame—
Liegemen to God and fathers of the free!

After all—
Hark! from the heights the clear, strong, clarion call
And the command imperious: "Stand forth,
Sons of the South and brothers of the North!
  Stand forth and be
  As one one soil and sea—
Your country's honor more than empire's worth!"

After all,
'Tis Freedom wears the loveliest coronal;
Her brow is to the morning; in the sod
She breathes the breath of patriots; every clod
  Answers her call
  And rises like a wall
Against the foes of liberty and God!

LAND OF MY HEART

from *Ad Patriam*

William Dudley Foulke

Land of my heart,
What future is before thee? Shall it be
To lie at ease, content with thy bright past,
Heedless of all the world, till idleness
Relax thy limbs, and swollen with wealth and pride
Thou shalt abandon justice and the poor?
Or shalt thou, reawakened, scatter wide
The glorious tidings of a liberty
That lifts the latch of opportunity
First to thy children—then to all mankind?
Love of my soul—God keep thee strong and pure,
That thou shalt be a fitting messenger
To carry hope to all the sons of men.

LAND OF THE FREE

Arthur Nicholas Hosking

AMERICA, O Power benign, great hearts revere your name,
You stretch your hand to every land, to weak and strong
the same;
You claim no conquest of the sea, nor conquest of the field,
But conquest for the rights of man, that despots all shall
yield.

Chorus:

America, far land of mine, home of the just and true,
All hail to thee, land of the free, and the Red-White-and-
Blue.

America, staunch, undismayed, your spirit is our might:
No splendor falls on feudal walls upon your mountain's
height,
But shafts of Justice pierce your skies to light the way for all,
A world's great brotherhood of man, that cannot, must not
fall.

America, in God we trust, we fear no tyrant's horde:
There's light that leads toward better deeds than conquest by
the sword;
Yet our cause is just, if fight we must until the world be
free
Of every menace, breed, or caste that strikes at Liberty.

America, home of the brave, our song in praise we bring—

Where Stars and Stripes the winds unfurl, 'tis there that
tributes ring;
Our fathers gave their lives that we should live in Freedom's
light—
Our lives we consecrate to thee, our guide the Might of
Right.

MY LAND

Thomas Osborne Davis

She is a rich and rare land;
Oh! she's a fresh and fair land,
She is a dear and rare land—
    This native land of mine.

No men than hers are braver—
Her women's hearts ne'er waver;
I'd freely die to save her,
    And think my lot divine.

She's not a dull or cold land;
No! she's a warm and bold land;
Oh! she's a true and old land—
    This native land of mine.

Could beauty ever guard her,
And virtue still reward her,
No foe would cross her border—
    No friend within it pine.

Oh! she's a fresh and fair land,
Oh! she's a true and rare land!
Yes, she's a rare and fair land—
    This native land of mine.

INNOMINATUS

from *The Lay of the Last Minstrel*

Sir Walter Scott

Breathes there a man with soul so dead,
Who never to himself hath said,
"This is my own, my native land!"
Whose heart hath ne'er within him burn'd
As home his footsteps he hath turn'd
From wandering on a foreign strand?
If such there breathe, go, mark him well;
For him no Minstrel raptures swell;
High though his titles, proud his name,
Boundless his wealth as wish can claim;
Despite those titles, power, and pelf,
The wretch, concentred all in self,
Living, shall forfeit fair renown,
And, doubly dying, shall go down
To the vile dust from whence he sprung,
Unwept, unhonour'd, and unsung.

THERE IS A LAND

James Montgomery

There is a land, of every land the pride,
Beloved by Heaven o'er all the world beside;
Where brighter suns dispense serener light,
And milder moons imparadise the night:
A land of beauty, virtue, valor, truth,
Time-tutored age, and love-exalted youth.
Where shall that land, that spot of earth, be found?
Art thou a man? A patriot? look around!
O! thou shalt find, howe'er thy footsteps roam,
That land thy country, and that spot thy home.

WHERE ARE YOU GOING, GREATHEART?

John Oxenham

Where are you going, Greatheart,
With your eager face and your fiery grace?
  Where are you going, Greatheart?

"To fight a fight with all my might,
For Truth and Justice, God and Right,
To grace all Life with His fair Light."
  Then God go with you, Greatheart!

Where are you going, Greatheart?
"To beard the Devil in his den;
To smite him with the strength of ten;
To set at large the souls of men."
  Then God go with you, Greatheart!

Where are you going, Greatheart?
"To cleanse the earth of noisome things;
To draw from life its poison stings;
To give free play to Freedom's wings."
  Then God go with you, Greatheart!

Where are you going, Greatheart?
"To lift Today above the Past;
To make Tomorrow sure and fast;
To nail God's colors to the mast."
  Then God go with you, Greatheart!

Where are you going, Greatheart?
"To break down old dividing lines;
To carry out my Lord's designs;
To build again His broken shrines."
 Then God go with you, Greatheart!

Where are you going, Greatheart?
"To set all burdened peoples free;
To win for all God's liberty;
To 'stablish His sweet sovereignty."
 God goeth with you, Greatheart!

THE GIFT OUTRIGHT

Robert Frost

The land was ours before we were the land's.
She was our land more than a hundred years
Before we were her people. She was ours
In Massachusetts, in Virginia;
But we were England's, still colonials,
Possessing what we still were unpossessed by,
Possessed by what we now no more possessed.
Something we were withholding made us weak
Until we found out that it was ourselves
We were withholding from our land of living,
And forthwith found salvation in surrender.
Such as we were we gave ourselves outright
(The deed of gift was many deeds of war)
To the land vaguely realizing westward,
But still unstoried, artless, unenhanced,
Such as she was, such as she would become.

AMERICA THE BEAUTIFUL

Katharine Lee Bates

O beautiful for spacious skies,
  For amber waves of grain,
For purple mountain majesties
  Above the fruited plain!
America! America!
  God shed His grace on thee
And crown thy good with brotherhood
  From sea to shining sea!

O beautiful for pilgrim feet,
  Whose stern, impassioned stress
A thoroughfare for freedom beat
  Across the wilderness!
America! America!
  God mend thine every flaw,
Confirm thy soul in self-control,
  Thy liberty in law!

O beautiful for heroes proved
  In liberating strife,
Who more than self their country loved,
  And mercy more than life!
America! America!
  May God thy gold refine,
Till all success be nobleness
  And every gain divine!

O beautiful for patriot dream
  That sees beyond the years
Thine alabaster cities gleam
  Undimmed by human tears!
America! America!
  God shed His grace on thee,
And crown thy good with brotherhood
  From sea to shining sea!

HAIL, COLUMBIA

Joseph Hopkinson

Hail! Columbia, happy land!
Hail! ye heroes, heaven-born band,
Who fought and bled in freedom's cause,
And when the storm of war was gone,
Enjoyed the peace your valor won;
Let independence be your boast,
Ever mindful what it cost,
Ever grateful for the prize,
Let its altar reach the skies.

Chorus:

> Firm, united let us be,
> Rallying round our liberty,
> As a band of brothers joined,
> Peace and safety we shall find.

Immortal patriots, rise once more!
Defend your rights, defend your shore;
Let no rude foe with impious hand,
Invade the shrine where sacred lies
Of toil and blood the well-earned prize;
While offering peace, sincere and just,
In heaven we place a manly trust,
That truth and justice will prevail,
And every scheme of bondage fail.

Sound, sound the trump of fame!
Let Washington's great name

Ring through the world with loud applause!
Let every clime to freedom dear
Listen with a joyful ear;
With equal skill, with steady power,
He governs in the fearful hour
Of horrid war, or guides with ease
The happier time of honest peace.

Behold the chief, who now commands,
Once more to serve his country stands,
The rock on which the storm will beat!
But armed in virtue, firm and true,
His hopes are fixed on heaven and you.
When hope was sinking in dismay,
When gloom obscured Columbia's day,
His steady mind, from changes free,
Resolved on death or liberty.

PLAIN-CHANT FOR AMERICA

Katherine Garrison Chapin

For the dream unfinished
Out of which we came,
We stand together,
While a hemisphere darkens
And the nations flame.

Our earth has been hallowed
With death for freedom;
Our walls have been hallowed
With freedom's thought.

Concord, Valley Forge, Harpers Ferry
Light up with their flares
Our sky of doubt.

We fear tyranny as our hidden enemy:
The black-shirt cruelty, the goose-step mind.

No dark signs close the doors of our speaking,
No bayonets bar the door to our prayers,
No gun butts shadow our children's eyes.

If we have failed—lynchings in Georgia,
Justice in Massachusetts undone,
The bloody fields of South Chicago—
Still a voice from the bruised and the battered
Speaks out in the light of a free sun.

Saying, "Tell them again, say it, America;
Say it again till it splits their ears:
Freedom is salt in our blood and its bone shape;
If freedom fails, we'll fight for more freedom—
This is the land, and these are the years!
When freedom's a whisper above their ashes
An obsolete word cut on their graves.
When the mind has yielded its last resistance,
And the last free flag is under the waves—

"Let them remember that here on the western
Horizon a star, once acclaimed, has not set;
And the strength of a hope, and the shape of a vision
Died for and sung for and fought for,
And worked for,
Is living yet."

TRIBUTE TO AMERICA

Percy Bysshe Shelley

There is a people mighty in its youth,
  A land beyond the oceans of the west,
Where, though with rudest rites, Freedom and Truth
  Are worshipt. From a glorious mother's breast,
  Who, since high Athens fell, among the rest
Sate like the Queen of Nations, but in woe,
  By inbred monsters outraged and opprest,
Turns to her chainless child for succor now,
It draws the milk of Power in Wisdom's fullest flow.

That land is like an eagle, whose young gaze
  Feeds on the noontide beam, whose golden plume
Floats moveless on the storm, and on the blaze
  Of sunrise gleams when Earth is wrapt in gloom;
  An epitaph of glory for thy tomb
Of murdered Europe may thy fame be made,
  Great People! As the sands shalt thou become;
Thy growth is swift as morn when night must fade;
The multitudinous Earth shall sleep beneath thy shade.

Yes, in the desert, there is built a home
  For Freedom! Genius is made strong to rear
The monuments of man beneath the dome
  Of a new Heaven; myriads assemble there
  Whom the proud lords of man, in rage or fear,
Drive from their wasted homes. The boon I pray
  Is this—that Cythna shall be convoyed there,--
Nay, start not at the name—America!

AMERICA

from *The National Ode, July 4, 1876*

Bayard Taylor

Foreseen in the vision of sages,
    Foretold when martyrs bled,
She was born of the longing of ages,
    By the truth of the noble dead
    And the faith of the living fed!
No blood in her lightest veins
Frets at remembered chains,
Nor shame of bondage has bowed her head.
    In her form and features still
    The unblenching Puritan will,
    Cavalier honor, Huguenot grace,
    The Quaker truth and sweetness,
  And the strength of the danger-girdled race
Of Holland, blend in a proud completeness.
From the homes of all, where her being began,
    She took what she gave to Man;
    Justice, that knew no station,
      Belief, as soul decreed,
    Free air for aspiration,
  Free force for independent deed!
    She takes, but to give again,
As the sea returns the rivers in rain;
And gathers the chosen of her seed
From the hunted of every crown and creed.
  Her Germany dwells by a gentler Rhine;
  Her Ireland sees the old sunburst shine;
  Her France pursues some dream divine;
  Her Norway keeps his mountain pine;

Her Italy waits by the western brine;
    And, broad-based under all,
Is planted England's oaken-hearted mood,
    As rich in fortitude
As e'er went worldward from the island wall!
    Fused in her candid light,
To one strong race all races here unite;
Tongues melt in hers, hereditary foremen
Forget their sword and slogan, kith and clan.
    'Twas glory, once, to be a Roman:
She makes it glory, now, to be a man!

AMERICA FOR ME

Henry van Dyke

'Tis fine to see the Old World, and travel up and down
Among the famous palaces and cities of renown,
To admire the crumbly castles and the statues of the
                                        kings,—
But now I think I've had enough of antiquated things.

  So it's home again, and home again, America for me!
  My heart is turning home again, and there I long to be
  In the land of youth and freedom beyond the ocean bars,
  Where the air is full of sunlight and the flag is full of
                                        stars.

Oh, London is a man's town, there's power in the air;
And Paris is a woman's town, with flowers in her hair;
And it's sweet to dream in Venice, and it's great to study
                                        Rome,
But when it comes to living, there is no place like home.

I like the German fir-woods, in green battalions drilled;
I like the gardens of Versailles with flashing fountains filled;
But, oh, to take your hand, my dear, and ramble for a day
In the friendly western woodland where Nature has her way!

I know that Europe's wonderful, yet something seems to lack!
The Past is too much with her, and the people looking back.
But the glory of the Present is to make the Future free,—
We love our land for what she is and what she is to be.

Oh, it's home again, and home again, America for me!
I want a ship that's westward bound to plough the rolling
sea,
To the blessed Land of Room Enough beyond the ocean
bars,
Where the air is full of sunlight and the flag is full of
stars.

NATIONAL HYMN

Daniel C. Roberts

God of our fathers, whose almighty hand
Leads forth in beauty all the starry band
Of shining worlds in splendor through the skies,
Our grateful songs before thy throne arise.

Thy love divine hath led us in the past,
In this free land by Thee our lot is cast;
Be Thou our ruler, guardian, guide, and stay,
Thy word our law, Thy paths our chosen way.

From war's alarms, from deadly pestilence,
Be Thy strong arm our ever-sure defense;
Thy true religion in our hearts increase,
Thy bounteous goodness nourish us in peace.

Refresh Thy people on their toilsome way,
Lead us from night to never-ending day;
Fill all our lives with love and grace divine,
And glory, laud and praise be ever Thine.

COLUMBUS

Joaquin Miller

Behind him lay the gray Azores,
  Behind the Gates of Hercules;
Before him not the ghost of shores,
  Before him only shoreless seas.
The good mate said: "Now must we pray
  For lo! the very stars are gone.
Brave Admiral, speak, what shall I say?"
  "Why, say 'Sail on! sail on! and on!'"

"My men grow mutinous day by day;
  My men grow ghastly wan and weak."
The stout mate thought of home; a spray
  Of salt wave washed his swarthy cheek.
"What shall I say, brave Admiral, say,
  If we sight naught but seas at dawn?"
"Why, you shall say at break of day,
  'Sail on! sail on! sail on! and on!'"

They sailed and sailed, as winds might blow,
  Until at last the blanched mate said:
"Why, now not even God would know
  Should I and all my men fall dead.
These very winds forget their way,
  For God from these dread seas is gone.
Now speak, brave Admiral, speak and say"—
  He said: "Sail on! sail on! and on!"

They sailed. They sailed. Then spake the mate:
  "This mad sea shows his teeth tonight.
He curls his lip, he lies in wait,
  With lifted teeth, as if to bite!
Brave Admiral, say but one good word:
  What shall we do when hope is gone?"
The words leapt like a leaping sword:
  "Sail on! sail on! sail on! and on!"

Then, pale and worn, he kept his deck,
  And peered through darkness. Ah, that night
Of all dark nights! And then a speck—
  A light! a light! a light! a light!
It grew, a starlit flag unfurled!
  It grew to be Time's burst of dawn.
He gained a world; he gave that world
  Its grandest lesson: "On! sail on!"

HENRY HUDSON'S QUEST 1609

Burton Egbert Stevenson

Out from the harbor of Amsterdam
    The Half Moon turned her prow to sea;
The coast of Norway dropped behind,
    Yet Northward still kept she
Through the drifting fog and the driving snow,
Where never before man dared to go:
"O Pilot, shall we find the strait that leads to the Eastern
                                 Sea?"
"A waste of ice before us lies—we must turn back," said he.

Westward they steered their tiny bark,
    Westward through weary weeks they sped,
Till the cold gray strand of a stranger-land
    Loomed through the mist ahead.
League after league they hugged the coast,
And their Captain never left his post:
"O Pilot, see you yet the strait that leads to the Eastern
                                 Sea?"
"I see but the rocks and the barren shore; no strait is there,"
                                   quoth he.

They sailed to the North—they sailed to the South—
    And at last they rounded an arm of sand
Which held the sea from a harbor's mouth—
    The loveliest in the land;
They kept their course across the bay,
And the shore before them fell away:

"O Pilot, see you not the strait that leads to the Eastern
                                                    Sea?"
"Hold the rudder true! Praise Christ Jesu! the strait is here,"
                                                    said he.

Onward they glide with wind and tide,
    Past marshes gray and crags sun-kissed;
They skirt the sills of green-clad hills,
    And meadows white with mist—
But alas! the hope and the brave, brave dream!
For rock and shallow bar the stream:
"O Pilot, can this be the strait that leads to the Eastern Sea?"
"Nay, Captain, nay; 'tis not this way; turn back we must,"
                                                    said he.

Full sad was Hudson's heart as he turned
    The Half Moon's prow to the South once more;
He saw no beauty in crag or hill,
    No beauty in curving shore;
For they shut him away from that fabled main
He sought his whole life along,—in vain:
"O Pilot, say, can there be a strait that leads to the Eastern
                                                    Sea?"
"God's crypt is sealed! 'Twill stand revealed in His own
                        good time," quoth he.

45

POCAHONTAS

William Makepeace Thackeray

Wearied arm and broken sword
  Wage in vain the desperate fight;
Round him press a countless horde,
  He is but a single knight.
Hark! a cry of triumph shrill
  Through the wilderness resounds
  As, with twenty bleeding wounds,
Sinks the warrior, fighting still.

Now they heap the funeral pyre,
  And the torch of death they light;
Ah! 'tis hard to die by fire!
  Who shall shield the captive knight
Round the stake with fiendish cry
  Wheel and dance the savage crowd,
  Cold the victim's mien and proud,
And his breast is bared to die.

Who shall shield the fearless heart?
  Who avert the murderous blade?
From the throng with sudden start
  See, there springs an Indian maid.
Quick she stands before the knight:
  "Loose the chain, unbind the ring
  I am daughter of the king,
And I claim the Indian right!"

Dauntlessly aside she flings
  Lifted ax and thirsty knife,
Fondly to his heart she clings,
  And her bosom guards his life!
In the woods of Powhatan,
  Still 'tis told by Indian fires,
  How a daughter of their sires
Saved a captive Englishman.

THE WORD OF GOD TO LEYDEN CAME 1620

Jeremiah Eames Rankin

The word of God to Leyden came,
    Dutch town by Zuyder Zee:
Rise up, my children of no name,
    My kings and priests to be.
There is an empire in the West,
    Which I will soon unfold;
A thousand harvests in her breast,
    Rocks ribbed with iron and gold.

Rise up, my children, time is ripe!
    Old things are passed away.
Bishops and kings from earth I wipe;
    Too long they've had their day.
A little ship have I prepared
    To bear you o'er the seas;
And in your souls, my will declared,
    Shall grow by slow degrees.

Beneath my throne the martyrs cry:
    I hear their voice, How long?
It mingles with their praises high,
    And with their victor song.
The thing they longed and waited for,
    But died without the sight;
So, this shall be! I wrong abhor,
    The world I'll now set right.

Leave, then, the hammer and the loom,
  You've other work to do;
For Freedom's commonwealth there's room,
  And you shall build it too.
I'm tired of bishops and their pride,
  I'm tired of kings as well;
Henceforth I take the people's side,
  And with the people dwell.

Tear off the mitre from the priest,
  And from the king, his crown;
Let all my captives be released;
  Lift up, whom men cast down.
Their pastors let the people choose,
  And choose their rulers too;
Whom they select, I'll not refuse,
  But bless the work they do.

The Pilgrims rose, at this, God's word,
  And sailed the wintry seas:
With their own flesh nor blood conferred,
  Nor thought of wealth or ease.
They left the towers of Leyden town,
  They left the Zuyder Zee;
And where they cast their anchor down,
  Rose Freedom's realm to be.

THE LANDING OF THE PILGRIM FATHERS IN NEW ENGLAND

Felicia D. Hemans

The breaking waves dashed high
  On a stern and rock-bound coast,
And the woods against a stormy sky
  Their giant branches tossed:

And the heavy night hung dark
  The hills and waters o'er,
When a band of exiles moored their bark
  On the wild New England shore.

Not as the conqueror comes,
  They, the true-hearted, came;
Not with the roll of the stirring drums,
  And the trumpet that sings of fame:

Not as the flying come,
  In silence and in fear;
They shook the depths of the desert gloom
  With their hymns of lofty cheer.

Amidst the storm they sang,
  And the stars heard, and the sea;
And the sounding aisles of the dim woods rang
  To the anthem of the free.

The ocean eagle soared
  From his nest by the white wave's foam,
And the rocking pines of the forest roared,—
  This was their welcome home.

There were men with hoary hair
  Amidst that pilgrim-band:
Why had they come to wither there,
  Away from their childhood's land?

There was woman's fearless eye,
  Lit by her deep love's truth;
There was manhood's brow serenely high,
  And the fiery heart of youth.

What sought they thus afar?
  Bright jewels of the mine?
The wealth of seas, the spoils of war?—
  They sought a faith's pure shrine!

Ay, call it holy ground,
  The soil where first they trod;
They have left unstained what there they found,—
  Freedom to worship God.

FIRST THANKSGIVING OF ALL

Nancy Byrd Turner

Peace and Mercy and Jonathan,
And Patience (very small),
Stood by the table giving thanks
The first Thanksgiving of all.
There was very little for them to eat,
Nothing special and nothing sweet;
Only bread and a little broth,
And a bit of fruit (and no tablecloth);
But Peace and Mercy and Jonathan
And Patience, in a row,
Stood up and asked a blessing on
Thanksgiving, long ago.
Thankful they were their ship had come
Safely across the sea;
Thankful they were for hearth and home,
And kin and company;
They were glad of broth to go with their bread,
Glad their apples were round and red,
Glad of mayflowers they would bring
Out of the woods again next spring.
So Peace and Mercy and Jonathan,
And Patience (very small),
Stood up gratefully giving thanks
The first Thanksgiving of all.

THE STAR-SPANGLED BANNER

Francis Scott Key

Oh, say, can you see, by the dawn's early light,
   What so proudly we hailed at the twilight's last gleaming,
Whose broad stripes and bright stars
   through the perilous fight,
   O'er the ramparts we watched were so gallantly streaming?
And the rockets' red glare, the bombs bursting in air,
Gave proof thro' the night that our flag was still there.
Oh, say, does that star-spangled banner yet wave
O'er the land of the free, and the home of the brave?

On the shore, dimly seen thro' the mists of the deep,
   Where the foe's haughty host in dread silence reposes,
What is that which the breeze o'er the towering steep,
   As it fitfully blows, half conceals, half discloses?
Now it catches the gleam of the morning's first beam,
In full glory reflected, now shines on the stream.
'Tis the star-spangled banner; oh, long may it wave
O'er the land of the free, and the home of the brave!

And where is that band who so vauntingly swore
   That the havoc of war and the battle's confusion
A home and a country should leave us no more?
   Their blood has washed out their foul footsteps' pollution.
No refuge could save the hireling and slave
From the terror of flight, or the gloom of the grave:
And the star-spangled banner in triumph doth wave
O'er the land of the free, and the home of the brave!

Oh, thus be it ever when freemen shall stand
    Between their loved homes and the war's desolation;
Blest with victory and peace, may the heaven-rescued land
    Praise the power that hath made and preserved us a nation!
Then conquer we must, when our cause it is just,
And this be our motto: "In God is our trust!"
And the star-spangled banner in triumph doth wave,
O'er the land of the free, and the home of the brave!

THE AMERICAN FLAG

Joseph Rodman Drake

When Freedom, from her mountain height,
 Unfurled her standard to the air,
She tore the azure robe of night,
 And set the stars of glory there!
She mingled with its gorgeous dyes
The milky baldric of the skies,
And striped its pure, celestial white
With streakings of the morning light;
Then, from his mansion in the sun,
She called her eagle-bearer down,
And gave into his mighty hand
The symbol of her chosen land!

Majestic monarch of the cloud!
 Who rear'st aloft thy regal form,
To hear the tempest trumping loud,
And see the lightning lances driven,
 When strive the warriors of the storm,
And rolls the thunder-drum of heaven,—
Child of the Sun! to thee 'tis given
 To guard the banner of the free,
To hover in the sulphur smoke,
To ward away the battle-stroke,
And bid its blending shine afar,
Like rainbows on the cloud of war,
 The harbingers of victory!

Flag of the brave! thy folds shall fly,
The sign of hope and triumph high!

When speaks the signal-trumpet tone,
And the long line comes gleaming on,
Ere yet the life-blood, warm and wet,
Has dimmed the glistening bayonet,
Each soldier's eye shall brightly turn
To where thy sky-born glories burn,
And, as his springing steps advance,
Catch war and vengeance from the glance.

And when the cannon-mouthings loud
Heave in wild wreaths the battle shroud,
And gory sabres rise and fall
Like shoots of flame on midnight's pall,
Then shall thy meteor glances glow,
   And cowering foes shall shrink beneath
Each gallant arm that strikes below
   That lovely messenger of death.

Flag of the seas! on ocean wave
Thy stars shall glitter o'er the brave;
When death, careering on the gale,
Sweeps darkly round the bellied sail,
And frightened waves rush wildly back
Before the broadside's reeling rack,
Each dying wanderer of the sea
Shall look at once to heaven and thee,
And smile to see thy splendors fly
In triumph o'er his closing eye.

Flag of the free heart's hope and home,
   By angel hands to valor given!
Thy stars have lit the welkin dome,
   And all thy hues were born in heaven.
Forever float that standard sheet!
   Where breathes the foe but falls before us,
With Freedom's soil beneath our feet,
   And Freedom's banner streaming o'er us!

A TOAST TO THE FLAG

John Jay Daly

Here's to the Red of it—
   There's not a thread of it,
   No, nor a shred of it
In all the spread of it
   From foot to head
But heroes bled for it,
Faced steel and lead for it,
Precious blood shed for it,
   Bathing it Red!

Here's to the White of it—
   Thrilled by the sight of it,
   Who knows the right of it
   But feels the might of it
      Through day and night?
   Womanhood's care for it
   Made manhood dare for it;
   Purity's pray'r for it
      Keeps it so White!

Here's to the Blue of it—
   Beauteous view of it,
   Heavenly hue of it,
   Star-spangled dew of it
      Sparkling anew;
   Diadems gleam for it,
   States stand supreme for it,
   Liberty's beam for it
      Brightens the Blue!

Here's to the Whole of it—
   Stars, stripes and pole of it,
   Body and soul of it,
   O, and the roll of it,
     Sun shining through;
   Hearts in accord for it
   Swear by the sword for it,
   Thanking the Lord for it,
     Red, White and Blue!

THE OLD FLAG

H. C. Bunner

Off with your hat as the flag goes by!
   And let the heart have its say;
You're man enough for a tear in your eye
   That you will not wipe away.

You're man enough for a thrill that goes
   To your very finger tips;
Ay! the lump just then in your throat that rose
   Spoke more than your parted lips.

Lift up the boy on your shoulder high,
   And show him the faded shred;
Those stripes would be red as the sunset sky
   If death could have dyed them red.

Off with your hat as the flag goes by!
   Uncover the youngster's head;
Teach him to hold it holy and high
   For the sake of its sacred dead.

COLUMBIA, THE GEM OF THE OCEAN

(first sung in Philadelphia about 1843)

Author Unknown

O Columbia, the gem of the ocean,
  The home of the brave and the free,
The shrine of each patriot's devotion,
  A world offers homage to thee.
Thy mandates make heroes assemble
  When Liberty's form stands in view;
Thy banners make tyranny tremble
    When borne by the red, white and blue.
      When borne by the red, white and blue,
      When borne by the red, white and blue,
      Thy banners make tyranny tremble
      When borne by the red, white and blue.

When war winged its wide desolation
  And threatened the land to deform,
The ark then of freedom's foundation,
  Columbia, rode safe thro' the storm:
With the garlands of vict'ry around her,
  When so proudly she bore her brave crew,
With her flag proudly floating before her,
  The boast of the red, white and blue.
The boast of the red, white and blue,
The boast of the red, white and blue,
With her flag proudly floating before her,
The boast of the red, white and blue.

The star-spangled banner bring hither,
   O'er Columbia's true sons let it wave;
May the wreaths they have won never wither,
   Nor its stars cease to shine on the brave:
May the service, united, ne'er sever,
   But hold to their colors so true;
The army and navy forever,
   Three cheers for the red, white and blue.
      Three cheers for the red, white and blue,
      Three cheers for the red, white and blue,
      The army and navy forever,
      Three cheers for the red, white and blue.

THE FLAG GOES BY

Henry Holcomb Bennett

Hats off!
Along the street there comes
A blare of bugles, a ruffle of drums,
A flash of color beneath the sky:
Hats off!
The flag is passing by!

Blue and crimson and white it shines,
Over the steel-tipped, ordered lines.
Hats off!
The colors before us fly;
But more than the flag is passing by:
Sea-fights and land-fights, grim and great,
Fought to make and to save the State;
Weary marches and sinking ships;
Cheers of victory on dying lips;

Days of plenty and years of peace;
March of a strong land's swift increase;
Equal justice, right and law,
Stately honor and reverend awe;
Sign of a nation great and strong
To ward her people from foreign wrong;
Pride and glory and honor—all
Live in the colors to stand or fall.

Hats off!
Along the street there comes
A blare of bugles, a ruffle of drums;
And loyal hearts are beating high:
Hats off!
The flag is passing by!

FREEDOM

Joel Barlow

Sun of the moral world; effulgent source
Of man's best wisdom and his steadiest force,
Soul-searching Freedom! here assume thy stand,
And radiate hence to every distant land;
Point out and prove how all the scenes of strife,
The shock of states, the impassion'd broils of life,
Spring from unequal sway; and how they fly
Before the splendor of thy peaceful eye;
Unfold at last the genuine social plan,
The mind's full scope, the dignity of man,
Bold nature bursting through her long disguise,
And nations daring to be just and wise.
Yes! righteous Freedom, heaven and earth and sea
Yield or withhold their various gifts for thee;
Protected Industry beneath thy reign
Leads all the virtues in her filial train;
Courageous Probity, with brow serene,
And Temperance calm presents her placid mien;
Contentment, Moderation, Labor, Art,
Mold the new man and humanize his heart:
To public plenty private ease dilates,
Domestic peace to harmony of states.
Protected Industry, careering far,
Detects the cause and cures the rage of war,
And sweeps, with forceful arm, to their last graves,
Kings from the earth and pirates from the waves.

A NATION'S STRENGTH

Ralph Waldo Emerson

What makes a nation's pillars high
  And its foundations strong?
What makes it mighty to defy
  The foes that round it throng?

It is not gold. Its kingdoms grand
  Go down in battle shock;
Its shafts are laid on sinking sand,
  Not on abiding rock.

Is it the sword? Ask the red dust
  Of empires passed away;
The blood has turned their stones to rust,
  Their glory to decay.

And is it pride? Ah, that bright crown
  Has seemed to nations sweet;
But God has struck its luster down
  In ashes at his feet.

Not gold but only men can make
  A people great and strong;
Men who for truth and honor's sake
  Stand fast and suffer long.

Brave men who work while others sleep,
  Who dare while others fly—
They build a nation's pillars deep
  And lift them to the sky.

ON FREEDOM

James Russell Lowell

They are slaves who fear to speak
For the fallen and the weak;
They are slaves who will not choose
Hatred, scoffing, and abuse,
Rather than in silence shrink
From the truth they needs must think;
They are slaves who dare not be
In the right with two or three.

OUR FATHERS FOUGHT FOR LIBERTY

James Russell Lowell

Our fathers fought for liberty,
They struggled long and well,
History of their deeds can tell—
But did they leave us free?

Are we free to speak our thought,
To be happy and be poor,
Free to enter Heaven's door,
To live and labor as we ought?

Are we then made free at last
From the fear of what men say.
Free to reverence today,
Free from the slavery of the past?

Our fathers fought for liberty,
They struggled long and well,
History of their deeds can tell—
But *ourselves* must set us free.

ONCE TO EVERY MAN AND NATION

from *The Present Crisis*

James Russell Lowell

. . . Once to every man and nation comes the moment to
decide,
In the strife of Truth with Falsehood, for the good or evil
side;
Some great cause, God's new Messiah, offering each the
bloom or blight,
Parts the goats upon the left hand, and the sheep upon the
right,
And the choice goes by forever 'twixt that darkness and that
light.

Hast thou chosen, O my people, on whose party thou shalt
stand,
Ere the Doom from its worn sandals shakes the dust against
our land?
Though the cause of Evil prosper, yet 'tis Truth alone is
strong,
And, albeit she wander outcast now, I see around her throng
Troops of beautiful, tall angels, to enshield her from all
wrong.

Careless seems the great Avenger; history's pages but record
One death-grapple in the darkness 'twixt old systems and the
Word;
Truth forever on the scaffold, Wrong forever on the throne—

Yet that scaffold sways the future, and behind the dim
                                                  unknown,
Standeth God within the shadow, keeping watch above his
                                                      own.

Then to side with Truth is noble when we share her
                                        wretched crust,
Ere her cause bring fame and profit, and 'tis prosperous to
                                                  be just;
Then it is the brave man chooses, while the coward stands
                                                    aside,
Doubting in his abject spirit, till his Lord is crucified,
And the multitude make virtue of the faith they had denied.

New occasions teach new duties; Time makes ancient good
                                                  uncouth;
They must upward still, and onward, who would keep abreast
                                                of Truth;
Lo! before us gleam her campfires! we ourselves must
                                            Pilgrims be,
Launch our Mayflower, and steer boldly through the
                                      desperate winter sea,
Nor attempt the Future's portal with the Past's blood-rusted
                                                      key.

GOD SAVE OUR PRESIDENT

Francis DeHaes Janvier

All hail! Unfurl the Stripes and Stars!
  The banner of the free!
Ten times ten thousand patriots greet
  The shrine of Liberty!
Come, with one heart, one hope, one aim,
  An undivided band,
To elevate, with solemn rites,
  The ruler of our land!

Not to invest a potentate
  With robes of majesty,—
Not to confer a kingly crown,
  Nor bend a subject knee.
We bow beneath no sceptred sway,
  Obey no royal nod:—
Columbia's sons, erect and free,
  Kneel only to their God!

Our ruler boasts no titled rank,
  No ancient, princely line,—
No regal right to sovereignty,
  Ancestral and divine.
A patriot,—at his country's call,
  Responding to her voice;
One of the people,—he becomes
  A sovereign by our choice!

And now, before the mighty pile,
  We've reared to Liberty,
He swears to cherish and defend
  The charter of the free!
God of our country! seal his oath
  With Thy supreme assent.
God save the Union of the States!
  God save our President!

THE ERRAND IMPERIOUS

Edwin Markham

But harken, my America, my own,
   Great Mother with the hill-flower in your hair!
Diviner is that light you bear alone,
   That dream that keeps your face forever fair.

'Tis yours to bear the World-State in your dream;
   To strike down Mammon and his brazen breed;
To build the Brother-Future, beam on beam—
   Yours, mighty one, to shape the mighty deed.

The armed heavens lean down to hear your fame,
   America: rise to your highborn part:
The thunders of the sea are in your name,
   The splendors of the sunrise in your heart.

OH MOTHER OF A MIGHTY RACE

William Cullen Bryant

Oh mother of a mighty race,
Yet lovely in thy youthful grace!
The elder dames, thy haughty peers,
Admire and hate thy blooming years.
   With words of shame
And taunts of scorn they join thy name.

For on thy cheeks the glow is spread
That tints thy morning hills with red;
Thy step—the wild deer's rustling feet
Within thy woods are not more fleet;
   Thy hopeful eye
Is bright as thine own sunny sky.

Ay, let them rail—those haughty ones,
While safe thou dwellest with thy sons.
They do not know how loved thou art,
How many a fond and fearless heart
   Would rise to throw
Its life between thee and the foe.

They know not, in their hate and pride,
What virtues with thy children bide;
How true, how good, thy graceful maids
Make bright, like flowers, the valley-shades;
   What generous men
Spring, like thine oaks, by hill and glen;—

What cordial welcomes greet the guest
By thy lone rivers of the West.
How faith is kept, and truth revered,
And man is loved, and God is feared,
  In woodland homes,
And where the ocean border foams.

There's freedom at thy gates and rest
For Earth's downtrodden and oppressed,
A shelter for the hunted head.
For the starved laborer toil and bread.
  Power, at thy bounds,
Stops and calls back his baffled hounds.

Oh, fair young mother! on thy brow
Shall sit a nobler grace than now.
Deep in the brightness of the skies
The thronging years in glory rise.
  And, as they fleet,
Drop strength and riches at thy feet.

A TOAST TO OUR NATIVE LAND

Robert Bridges

Huge and alert, irascible yet strong,
We make our fitful way 'mid right and wrong.
One time we pour out millions to be free,
Then rashly sweep an empire from the sea!
One time we strike the shackles from the slaves,
And then, quiescent, we are ruled by knaves.
Often we rudely break restraining bars,
And confidently reach out toward the stars.

Yet under all there flows a hidden stream
Sprung from the Rock of Freedom, the great dream
Of Washington and Franklin, men of old
Who knew that Freedom is not bought with gold.
This is the Land we love, our heritage,
Strange mixture of the gross and fine, yet sage
And full of promise—destined to be great.
Drink to Our Native Land! God Bless the State!

BOSTON HYMN

(Read in Boston Music Hall, January 1, 1863)

Ralph Waldo Emerson

The word of the Lord by night
To the watching Pilgrims came,
As they sat by the seaside,
And filled their hearts with flame.

God said, I am tired of kings,
I suffer them no more;
Up to my ear the morning brings
The outrage of the poor.

Think ye I made this ball
A field of havoc and war,
Where tyrants great and tyrants small
Might harry the weak and poor?

My angel, his name is Freedom—
Choose him to be your king;
He shall cut pathways east and west,
And fend you with his wing.

Lo! I uncover the land
Which I hid of old time in the West,
As the sculptor uncovers the statue
When he has wrought his best;

I show Columbia, of the rocks
Which dip their foot in the seas,
And soar to the airborne flocks
Of clouds, and the boreal fleece.

I will divide my goods;
Call in the wretch and slave:
None shall rule but the humble,
And none but toil shall have.

I will have never a noble,
No lineage counted great;
Fishers and choppers and ploughmen
Shall constitute a state.

Go, cut down trees in the forest,
And trim the straightest boughs;
Cut down the trees in the forest,
And build me a wooden house.

Call the people together,
The young men and the sires,
The digger in the harvest field,
Hireling, and him that hires;

And here in a pine statehouse
They shall choose men to rule
In every needful faculty,
In church, and state, and school.

Lo, now! if these poor men
Can govern the land and sea,
And make just laws below the sun,
As planets faithful be.

And ye shall succor men;
'Tis nobleness to serve;
Help them who cannot help again:
Beware from right to swerve.

I break your bonds and masterships,
And I unchain the slave:
Free be his heart and hand henceforth
As wind and wandering wave.

I cause from every creature
His proper good to flow:
As much as he is and doeth,
So much he shall bestow.

But laying hands on another
To coin his labor and sweat,
He goes in pawn to his victim
For eternal years in debt.

Today unbind the captive
So only are ye unbound;
Lift up a people from the dust,
Trump of their rescue, sound!

Pay ransom to the owner,
And fill the bag to the brim.
Who is the owner? The slave is owner,
And ever was. Pay him.

Oh North! give him beauty for rags,
And honor, O South! for his shame;
Nevada! coin thy golden crags
With Freedom's image and name.

Up! And the dusky race
That sat in darkness long—
Be swift their feet as antelopes,
And as behemoth strong.

Come, East and West and North,
By races, as snowflakes,
And carry my purpose forth,
Which neither halts nor shakes.

My will fulfilled shall be,
For, in daylight or in dark,
My thunderbolt has eyes to see
His way home to the mark.

INDEPENDENCE BELL, July 4, 1776

Author Unknown

There was a tumult in the city
In the quaint old Quaker town,
And the streets were rife with people
Pacing restless up and down—
People gathering at corners,
Where they whispered each to each,
And the sweat stood on their temples
With the earnestness of speech.

As the bleak Atlantic currents
Lash the wild Newfoundland shore,
So they beat against the State House,
So they surged against the door;
And the mingling of their voices
Made the harmony profound,
Till the quiet street of Chestnut
Was all turbulent with sound.

"Will they do it?" "Dare they do it?"
"Who is speaking?" "What's the news?"
"What of Adams?" "What of Sherman?"
"Oh, God grant they won't refuse!"
"Make some way there!" "Let me nearer!"
"I am stifling!" "Stifle then!
When a nation's life's at hazard,
We've no time to think of men!"

So they surged against the State House,
While all solemnly inside,
Sat the Continental Congress,
Truth and reason for their guide,
O'er a simple scroll debating,
Which, though simple it might be,
Yet should shake the cliffs of England
With the thunders of the free.

Far aloft in that high steeple
Sat the bellman, old and gray,
He was weary of the tyrant
And his iron-sceptered sway;
So he sat, with one hand ready
On the clapper of the bell,
When his eye could catch the signal,
The long-expected news to tell.

See! See! The dense crowd quivers
Through all its lengthy line,
As the boy beside the portal
Hastens forth to give the sign!
With his little hands uplifted,
Breezes dallying with his hair,
Hark! with deep, clear intonation,
Breaks his young voice on the air.

Hushed the people's swelling murmur,
Whilst the boy crys joyously;
"Ring!" he shouts, "Ring! Grandpapa,
Ring! oh, ring for Liberty!"
Quickly, at the given signal
The old bellman lifts his hand,
Forth he sends the good news, making
Iron music through the land.

How they shouted! What rejoicing!
How the old bell shook the air,
Till the clang of freedom ruffled,
The calmly gliding Delaware!
How the bonfires and the torches
Lighted up the night's repose,
And from the flames, like fabled Phoenix,
Our glorious liberty arose!

That old State House bell is silent,
Hushed is now its clamorous tongue;
But the spirit it awakened
Still is living—ever young;
And when we greet the smiling sunlight
On the fourth of each July,
We will ne'er forget the bellman
Who, betwixt the earth and sky,
Rung out, loudly, "Independence";
Which, please God, shall never die!

THE FOURTH OF JULY

John Pierpont

Day of glory! Welcome day!
Freedom's banners greet thy ray;
See! how cheerfully they play
   With thy morning breeze,
On the rocks where pilgrims kneeled,
On the heights where squadrons wheeled,
When a tyrant's thunder pealed
   O'er the trembling seas.

God of armies! did thy stars
On their courses smite his cars;
Blast his arm, and wrest his bars
   From the heaving tide?
On our standards! lo! they burn.
And, when days like this return,
Sparkle o'er the soldier's urn
   Who for freedom died.

God of peace! whose spirit fills
All the echoes of our hills,
All the murmur of our rills,
   Now the storm is o'er,
O let freemen be our sons,
And let future Washingtons
Rise, to lead their valiant ones
   Till there's war no more!

ODE

(Sung in the Town Hall, Concord, July 4, 1857)

Ralph Waldo Emerson

O tenderly the haughty day
  Fills his blue urn with fire;
One morn is in the mighty heaven,
  And one in our desire.

The cannon booms from town to town,
  Our pulses beat no less,
The joy-bells chime their tidings down,
  Which children's voices bless.

For He that flung the broad blue fold
  O'er-mantling land and sea,
One third part of the sky unrolled
  For the banner of the free.

The men are ripe of Saxon kind
  They build an equal state,—
To take the statute from the mind
  And make of duty fate.

United States! the ages plead,—
  Present and Past in under-song,—
Go put your creed into your deed,
  Nor speak with double tongue.

For sea and land don't understand
  Nor skies without a frown

See rights for which the one hand fights
  By the other cloven down.

Be just at home; then write your scroll
  Of honor o'er the sea,
And bid the broad Atlantic roll
  A ferry of the free.

And henceforth there shall be no chain,
  Save underneath the sea
The wires shall murmur through the main
  Sweet songs of liberty.

The conscious stars accord above,
  The waters wild below,
And under, through the cable wove,
  Her fiery errands go.

For He that worketh high and wise,
  Nor pauses in his plan,
Will take the sun out of the skies
  Ere freedom out of man.

CENTENNIAL HYMN

John Greenleaf Whittier

I

Our father's God! from out whose hand
The centuries fall like grains of sand,
We meet to-day, united, free,
And loyal to our land and Thee,
To thank Thee for the era done,
And trust Thee for the opening one.

II

Here, where of old, by Thy design,
The fathers spake that word of Thine
Whose echo is the glad refrain
Of rended bolt and falling chain,
To grace our festal time, from all
The zones of earth our guests we call.

III

Be with us while the New World greets
The Old World thronging in its streets,
Unveiling all the triumphs won
By art or toil beneath the sun;
And unto common good ordain
This rivalship of hand and brain.

IV

Thou, who hast here in concord furled
The war flags of a gathered world,
Beneath our Western skies fulfill
The Orient's mission of good-will,
And, freighted with love's Golden Fleece,
Send back its Argonauts of peace.

V

For art and labor met in truce,
For beauty made the bride of use,
We thank Thee; but, withal, we crave
The austere virtues strong to save,
The honor proof to place or gold,
The manhood never bought nor sold!

VI

Oh make Thou us, through centuries long,
In peace secure, in justice strong;
Around our gift of freedom draw
The safeguards of Thy righteous law:
And, cast in some diviner mould,
Let the new cycle shame the old!

CENTENNIAL HYMN

John Pierpont

Break forth in song, ye trees,
As through your tops the breeze
  Sweeps from the sea;
For on its rushing wings,
To your cool shades and springs,
That breeze a people brings,
  Exiled, though free.

Ye sister hills, lay down
Of ancient oaks your crown,
  In homage due;
These are the great of earth—
Great, nor by kingly birth,
Great, in their well-proved worth,
  Firm hearts and true.

These are the living lights,
That, from your bold green heights,
  Shall shine afar,
Till they who name the name
Of Freedom, toward the flame
Come, as the Magi came
  Toward Bethlehem's star.

Gone are those great and good,
Who here, in peril stood
  And raised their hymn.

Peace to the reverend dead!
The light, that on their head
Two hundred years have shed,
   Shall ne'er grow dim.

Ye temples, that, to God,
Rise where our fathers trod,
   Guard well your trust:
The faith, that dared the sea,
The truth, that made them free,
Their cherished purity,
   Their garnered dust.

Thou high and holy One,
Whose care for sire and son
   All nature fills,
While day shall break and close,
While night her crescent shows
O, let thy light repose
   On these our hills.

A BALLAD OF THE BOSTON TEA-PARTY, December 16, 1773

Oliver Wendell Holmes

No! never such a draught was poured
  Since Hebe served with nectar
The bright Olympians and their Lord,
  Her over-kind protector,—
Since Father Noah squeezed the grape
  And took to such behaving
As would have shamed our grandsire ape
  Before the days of shaving,—
No! ne'er was mingled such a draught
  In palace, hall, or arbor,
As freeman brewed and tyrants quaffed
  That night in Boston Harbor!
It kept King George so long awake
  His brain at last got addled,
It made the nerves of Britain shake,
  With sevenscore millions saddled;
Before that bitter cup was drained
  Amid the roar of cannon,
The Western war-cloud's crimson stained
  The Thames, the Clyde, the Shannon;
Full many a six-foot grenadier
  The flattened grass had measured,
And many a mother many a year
  Her tearful memories treasured;
Fast spread the tempest's darkening pall,
  The mighty realms were troubled,
The storm broke loose, but first of all
  The Boston teapot bubbled!

An evening party,—only that,
  No formal invitation,
No gold-laced coat, no stiff cravat,
  No feast in contemplation,
No silk-robed dames, no fiddling band,
  No flowers, no songs, no dancing,—
A tribe of red men, axe in hand,—
  Behold the guests advancing!
How fast the stragglers join the throng,
  From stall and workshop gathered!
The lively barber skips along
  And leaves a chin half-lathered;
The smith has flung his hammer down,—
  The horseshoe still is glowing;
The truant tapster at the Crown
  Has left the beer-cask flowing;
The cooper's boys have dropped the adze,
  And trot behind their master;
Up run the tarry ship-yard lads,—
  The crowd is hurrying faster,—

Out from the Millpond's purlieus gush
  The streams of white-faced millers,
And down their slippery alleys rush
  The lusty young Fort-Hillers;
The ropewalk lends its 'prentice crew,—
  The tories seize the omen:
"Aye, boys, you'll soon have work to do
  For England's rebel foemen,
'King Hancock,' Adams, and their gang,
  That fire the mob with treason,—
When these we shoot and those we hang
  The town will come to reason."

Oh—on to where the tea-ships ride!
  And now their ranks are forming,—

A rush, and up the Dartmouth's side
   The Mohawk band is swarming!
See the fierce natives! What a glimpse
   Of paint and fur and feather,
As all at once the full-grown imps
   Light on the deck together!
A scarf the pigtail's secret keeps,
   A blanket hides the breeches,—
And out the cursed cargo leaps,
   And overboard it pitches!

O woman, at the evening board
   So gracious, sweet, and purring,
So happy while the tea is poured,
   So blest while spoons are stirring,
What martyr can compare with thee,
   The mother, wife, or daughter,
That night, instead of best Bohea,
   Condemned to milk and water!

Ah, little dreams the quiet dame
   Who plies with rock and spindle
The patient flax, how great a flame
   Yon little spark shall kindle!
The lurid morning shall reveal
   A fire no king can smother
Where British flint and Boston Steel
   Have clashed against each other!
Old charters shrivel in its track,
   His Worship's bench has crumbled,
It climbs and clasps the union-jack,
   Its blazoned pomp is humbled,
The flags go down on land and sea
   Like corn before the reapers;
So burned the fire that brewed the tea
   That Boston served her keepers!

The waves that wrought a century's wreck
  Have rolled o'er whig and tory;
The Mohawks on the Dartmouth's deck
  Still live in song and story;
The waters in the rebel bay
  Have kept the tea-leaf savor;
Our old North-Enders in their spray
  Still taste a Hyson flavor;
And Freedom's teacup still o'erflows
  With ever fresh libations,
To cheat of slumber all her foes
  And cheer the wakening nations!

PAUL REVERE'S RIDE

Henry Wadsworth Longfellow

Listen, my children, and you shall hear
Of the midnight ride of Paul Revere,
On the eighteenth of April, in Seventy-five;
Hardly a man is now alive
Who remembers that famous day and year.

He said to his friend, "If the British march
By land or sea from the town tonight,
Hang a lantern aloft in the belfry arch
Of the North Church tower as a signal light,—
One, if by land, and two, if by sea;
And I on the opposite shore will be,
Ready to ride and spread the alarm
Through every Middlesex village and farm,
For the country folk to be up and to arm."

Then he said, "Good night!" and with muffled oar
Silently rowed to the Charlestown shore,
Just as the moon rose over the bay,
Where swinging wide at her moorings lay
The Somerset, British man-of-war;
A phantom ship, with each mast and spar
Across the moon like a prison bar,
And a huge black hulk, that was magnified
By its own reflection in the tide.

Meanwhile, his friend, through alley and street,
Wanders and watches with eager ears,
Till in the silence around him he hears
The muster of men at the barrack door,
The sound of arms, and the tramp of feet,
And the measured tread of the grenadiers,
Marching down to their boats on the shore.

Then he climbed the tower of the Old North Church,
By the wooden stairs, with stealthy tread,
To the belfry-chamber overhead,
And startled the pigeons from their perch
On the somber rafters, that round him made
Masses and moving shapes of shade,—
By the trembling ladder, steep and tall,
To the highest window in the wall,
Where he paused to listen and look down
A moment on the roofs of the town,
And the moonlight flowing over all.

Beneath, in the churchyard, lay the dead,
In their night-encampment on the hill,
Wrapped in silence so deep and still
That he could hear, like a sentinel's tread,
The watchful night-wind, as it went
Creeping along from tent to tent,
And seeming to whisper, "All is well!"
A moment only he feels the spell
Of the place and the hour, and the secret dread
Of the lonely belfry and the dead;
For suddenly all his thoughts are bent
On a shadowy something far away,
Where the river widens to meet the bay,—
A line of black that blends and floats
On the rising tide, like a bridge of boats.

Meanwhile, impatient to mount and ride,
Booted and spurred, with a heavy stride
On the opposite shore walked Paul Revere.
Now he patted his horse's side,
Now gazed at the landscape far and near,
Then, impetuous, stamped the earth,
And turned and tightened his saddle-girth;
But mostly he watched with eager search
The belfry-tower of the Old North Church,
As it rose above the graves on the hill,
Lonely and spectral and somber and still.
And lo! as he looks, on the belfry's height
A glimmer, and then a gleam of light!
He springs to the saddle, the bridle he turns,
But lingers and gazes, till full on his sight
A second lamp in the belfry burns!

A hurry of hoofs in a village street,
A shape in the moonlight, a bulk in the dark,
And beneath, from the pebbles, in passing, a spark
Struck out by a steed flying fearless and fleet;
That was all! And yet, through the gloom and the light
The fate of a nation was riding that night;
And the spark struck out by that steed in his flight,
Kindled the land into flame with its heat.

He has left the village and mounted the steep,
And beneath him, tranquil and broad and deep,
Is the Mystic, meeting the ocean tides;
And under the alders, that skirt its edge,
Now soft on the sand, now loud on the ledge,
Is heard the tramp of his steed as he rides.

It was twelve by the village clock
When he crossed the bridge into Medford town.
He heard the crowing of the cock,

And the barking of the farmer's dog,
And felt the damp of the river fog,
That rises after the sun goes down.

It was one by the village clock,
When he galloped into Lexington.
He saw the gilded weathercock
Swim in the moonlight as he passed,
And the meeting-house windows, blank and bare,
Gaze at him with a spectral glare,
As if they already stood aghast
At the bloody work they would look upon.

It was two by the village clock,
When he came to the bridge in Concord town.
He heard the bleating of the flock,
And the twitter of birds among the trees,
And felt the breath of the morning breeze
Blowing over the meadows brown.
And one was safe and asleep in his bed
Who at the bridge would be first to fall,
Who that day would be lying dead,
Pierced by a British musket-ball.

You know the rest. In the books you have read,
How the British Regulars fired and fled,—
How the farmers gave them ball for ball,
From behind each fence and farmyard wall,
Chasing the redcoats down the lane,
Then crossing the fields to emerge again
Under the trees at the turn of the road,
And only pausing to fire and load.
So through the night rode Paul Revere;
And so through the night went his cry of alarm
To every Middlesex village and farm,—

A cry of defiance, and not of fear,
A voice in the darkness, a knock at the door,
And a word that shall echo forevermore!
For, borne on the night-wind of the Past,
Through all our history, to the last,
In the hour of darkness and peril and need,
The people will waken and listen to hear
The hurrying hoofbeats of that steed,
And the midnight message of Paul Revere.

CONCORD HYMN

(Sung at the completion of the Concord Monument, April 19, 1836)

Ralph Waldo Emerson

By the rude bridge that arched the flood,
  Their flag to April's breeze unfurled,
Here once the embattled farmers stood,
  And fired the shot heard round the world.

The foe long since in silence slept;
  Alike the conqueror silent sleeps;
And Time the ruined bridge has swept
  Down the dark stream which seaward creeps.

On this green bank, by this soft stream,
  We set to-day a votive stone;
That memory may their deed redeem,
  When, like our sires, our sons are gone.

Spirit, that made those heroes dare
  To die, and leave their children free,
Bid Time and Nature gently spare
  The shaft we raise to them and thee.

LEXINGTON, April 19, 1775

Sidney Lanier

O'er Cambridge set the yeoman's mark:
Climb, patriot, through the April dark.
O lanthorn! kindle fast thy light,
Thou budding star in the April night,
For never a star more news hath told,
Or later flame in heaven shall hold.
Ay, lanthorn on the North Church tower,
When that thy church hath had her hour,
Still from the top of Reverence high
Shalt thou illume Fame's ampler sky;
For, statured large o'er town and tree,
Time's tallest Figure stands by thee,
And, dim as now thy wick may shine,
The Future lights his lamp at thine.

Now haste thee while the way is clear,
    Paul Revere!
Haste, Dawes! but haste thou not, O Sun!
    To Lexington.

Then Devens looked and saw the light:
He got him forth into the night,
And watched alone on the river-shore,
And marked the British ferrying o'er.
John Parker! rub thine eyes and yawn,
But one o'clock and yet 't is Dawn!
Quick, rub thine eyes and draw thy hose:

The Morning comes ere darkness goes.
Have forth and call the yeomen out,
For somewhere, somewhere close about
Full soon a Thing must come to be
Thine honest eyes shall stare to see—
Full soon before thine patriot eyes
Freedom from out of a Wound shall rise.

Then haste ye, Prescott and Revere!
Bring all the men of Lincoln here;
Let Chelmsford, Littleton, Carlisle,
Let Acton, Bedford, hither file—
Oh hither file, and plainly see
Out of a wound leap Liberty.
Say, Woodman April! all in green,
Say, Robin April! hast thou seen
In all thy travel round the earth
Ever a morn of calmer birth?
But Morning's eye alone serene
Can gaze across yon village-green
To where the trooping British run
    Through Lexington.

Good men in fustian, stand ye still;
The men in red come o'er the hill.
Lay down your arms, damned Rebels! cry
The men in red full haughtily.
But never a grounding gun is heard;
The men in fustian stand unstirred;
Dead calm, save maybe a wise bluebird
Puts in his little heavenly word.
O men in red! if ye but knew
The half as much as bluebirds do,
Now in the little tender calm
Each hand would out, and every palm
With patriot palm strike brotherhood's stroke
Or ere these lines of battle broke.

O men in red! if ye but knew
The least of all that bluebirds do,
Now in this little godly calm
Yon voice might sing the Future's Psalm—
The Psalm of Love with the brotherly eyes
Who pardons and is very wise—
Yon voice that shouts, high-hoarse with ire,
      Fire!
The red-coats fire, the homespuns fall:
The homespuns' anxious voices call,
Brother, art hurt? and *Where hit, John?*
And, *Wipe this blood,* and *Men, come on,*
And, *Neighbor, do but lift my head,*
And, *Who is wounded? Who is dead?*
Seven are killed. My God! my God!
Seven lie dead on the village sod.
Two Harringtons, Parker, Hadley, Brown,
Monroe and Porter,—these are down.
Nay, look! Stout Harrington not yet dead!
He crooks his elbow, lifts his head.
He lies at the step of his own house-door;
He crawls and makes a path of gore.
The wife from the window hath seen, and rushed;
He hath reached the step, but the blood hath gushed;
He hath crawled to the step of his own house-door,
But his head hath dropped: he will crawl no more.
Clasp, Wife, and kiss, and lift the head:
Harrington lies at his doorstep dead.

But, O ye Six that round him lay
And bloodied up that April day!
As Harrington fell, ye likewise fell—
At the door of the House wherein ye dwell;
As Harrington came, ye likewise came
And died at the door of your House of Fame.

NEW ENGLAND'S CHEVY CHASE,
April 19, 1775

Edward Everett Hale

'Twas the dead of the night. By the pineknot's red light
  Brooks lay, half asleep, when he heard the alarm—
Only this, and no more, from a voice at the door:
  "The Redcoats are out, and have passed Phips's farm."

Brooks was booted and spurred; he said never a word:
  Took the horn from its peg, and his gun from the rack;
To the cold midnight air he led out his white mare,
  Strapped the girths and the bridle, and sprang to her back.

Up the North County road at her full pace she strode,
  Till Brooks reined her up at John Tarbell's to say,
"We have got the alarm—they have left Phips's farm;
  You rouse the East Precinct, and I'll go this way."

John called his hired man, and they harnessed the span;
  They roused Abram Garfield, and Abram called me:
"Turn out right away; let no minuteman stay;
  The Redcoats have landed at Phips's," says he.

By the Powder House Green seven others fell in;
  At Nahum's the men from the Sawmill came down;
So that when Jabez Bland gave the word of command,
  And said, "Forward, march!" there marched forward THE
                                    TOWN.

Parson Wilderspin stood by the side of the road,
  And took off his hat, and he said, "Let us pray!
O Lord, God of might, let Thine angels of light
  Lead Thy children tonight to the glories of day!
And let Thy stars fight all the foes of the Right
  As the stars fought of old against Sisera."

And from heaven's high arch those stars blessed our march,
  Till the last of them faded in twilight away;
And with morning's bright beam, by the banks of the stream
  Half the county marched in, and we heard Davis say:

"On the King's own highway I may travel all day,
  And no man hath warrant to stop me," says he;
"I've no man that's afraid, and I'll march at their head."
  Then he turned to the boys, "Forward, march! Follow me."

And we marched as he said, and the Fifer he played
  The old "White Cockade," and he played it right well.
We saw Davis fall dead, but no man was afraid;
  That bridge we'd have had, though a thousand men fell.

This opened the play, and it lasted all day.
  We made Concord too hot for the Redcoats to stay;
Down the Lexington way we stormed, black, white, and gray
  We were first in the feast, and were last in the fray.

They would turn in dismay, as red wolves turn at bay.
  They leveled, they fired, they charged up the road.
Cephas Willard fell dead; he was shot in the head
  As he knelt by Aunt Prudence's well sweep to load.

John Danforth was hit just in Lexington Street,
  John Bridge at that lane where you cross Beaver Falls,
And Winch and the Snows just above John Munroe's—
  Swept away by one swoop of the big cannonballs.

I took Bridge on my knee, but he said, "Don't mind me;
Fill your horn from mine—let me lie where I be.
Our fathers," says he, "that their sons might be free,
Left their king on his throne, and came over the sea;
And that man is a knave, or a fool who, to save
His life for a minute, would live like a slave."

Well, all would not do! There were men good as new—
From Rumford, from Saugus, from towns far away—
Who filled up quick and well for each soldier that fell;
And we drove them, and drove them, and drove them,
all day.
We knew, every one, it was war that begun,
When that morning's marching was only half done.

In the hazy twilight, at the coming of night,
I crowded three buckshot and one bullet down.
'Twas my last charge of lead; and I aimed her and said,
"Good luck to you, lobsters, in old Boston Town."

In a barn at Milk Row, Ephraim Bates and Munroe,
And Baker, and Abram, and I made a bed.
We had mighty sore feet, and we'd nothing to eat;
But we'd driven the Redcoats, and Amos, he said:
"It's the first time," says he, "that it's happened to me
To march to the sea by this road where we've come;
But confound this whole day, but we'd all of us say
We'd rather have spent it this way than to home."

The hunt had begun with the dawn of the sun,
And night saw the wolf driven back to his den.
And never since then, in the memory of men,
Has the Old Bay State seen such a hunting again.

WARREN'S ADDRESS AT BUNKER HILL, June 16, 1775

John Pierpont

Stand! the ground's your own, my braves!
Will ye give it up to slaves?
Will ye look for greener graves?
  Hope ye mercy still?
What's the mercy despots feel?
Hear it in that battle-peal!
Read it on yon bristling steel!
  Ask it—ye who will.

Fear ye foes who kill for hire?
Will ye to your homes retire?
Look behind you!—they're afire!
  And, before you, see
Who have done it! From the vale
On they come—and will ye quail?
Leaden rain and iron hail
  Let their welcome be!

In the God of battles trust!
Die we may—and die we must:
But, O, where can dust to dust
  Be consigned so well,
As where heaven its dews shall shed
On the martyred patriot's bed,
And the rocks shall raise their head,
  Of his deeds to tell?

YANKEE DOODLE

Edward Bangs

Father and I went down to camp,
  Along with Captain Gooding,
And there we see the men and boys,
  As thick as hasty pudding.

Chorus:

Yankee Doodle, keep it up,
  Yankee Doodle, dandy,
Mind the music and the step,
  And with the girls be handy.

And there we see a thousand men,
  As rich as Squire David;
And what they wasted every day
  I wish it could be saved.

The 'lasses they eat every day
  Would keep our house a winter;
They have so much that, I'll be bound,
  They eat whene'er they're a mind to.

And there we see a swamping gun,
  As big as a log of maple,
Upon a deuced little cart,
  A load for father's cattle.

And every time they shoot it off,
  It takes a horn of powder,
And makes a noise like father's gun,
  Only a nation louder.

I went as nigh to one myself
  As Siah's underpinning;
And father went as nigh again,
  I thought the deuce was in him.

Cousin Simon grew so bold,
  I thought he would have cocked it,
It scared me so I shrinked it off,
  And hung by father's pocket.

And Captain Davis had a gun,
  He kind of clapped his hand on't,
And stuck a crooked stabbing-iron
  Upon the little end on't.

And there I see a pumpkin shell
  As big as mother's basin;
And every time they touched it off,
  They scampered like the nation.

I see a little barrel, too,
  The heads were made of leather,
They knocked upon't with little clubs
  To call the folks together.

And there was Captain Washington,
  And gentlefolks about him,
They say he's grown so tarnal proud
  He will not ride without 'em.

He had got on his meeting clothes,
  And rode a strapping stallion,
And gave his orders to the men—
  I guess there was a million.

The flaming ribbons in his hat,
  They looked so tearing fine ah,
I wanted peskily to get,
  To give to my Jemima.

And then I see a snarl of men
  A digging graves, they told me.
So tarnal long, so tarnal deep,
  They 'tended they should hold me.

It scared me so, I hooked it off,
  Nor stopped, as I remember,
Nor turned about, till I got home,
  Locked up in mother's chamber.

NATHAN HALE

William Ordway Partridge

One hero dies,—a thousand new ones rise,
  As flowers are sown where perfect blossoms fall,—
Then quite unknown,—the name of Hale now cries
  Where duty sounds her silent call;

With head erect he moves, and stately pace,
  To meet an awful doom,—no ribald jest
Brings scorn or hate to that exalted face,
  His thoughts are far away, poised and at rest;

Now on the scaffold see him turn and bid
  Farewell to home and all his heart holds dear,
Majestic presence,—all men's weakness hid,
  And all his strength in that one hour made clear,—
"I have one last regret,—that is to give
But one poor life, that my own land may live!"

NATHAN HALE

Francis Miles Finch

To drumbeat, and heartbeat,
  A soldier marches by;
There is color in his cheek,
  There is courage in his eye,
Yet to drumbeat and heartbeat
  In a moment he must die.

By the starlight and moonlight,
  He seeks the Briton's camp;
He hears the rustling flag,
  And the armed sentry's tramp;
And the starlight and moonlight
  His silent wanderings lamp.

With slow tread and still tread,
  He scans the tented line;
And he counts the battery guns,
  By the gaunt and shadowy pine;
And his slow tread and still tread
  Gives no warning sign.

The dark wave, the plumed wave,
  It meets his eager glance;
And it sparkles 'neath the stars,
  Like the glimmer of a lance—
A dark wave, a plumed wave,
  On an emerald expanse.

A sharp clang, a steel clang,
　　And terror in the sound!
For the sentry, falcon-eyed,
　　In the camp a spy hath found;
With a sharp clang, a steel clang,
　　The patriot is bound.

With calm brow, and steady brow,
　　He listens to his doom;
In his look there is no fear,
　　Nor a shadow-trace of gloom;
But with calm brow and steady brow,
　　He robes him for the tomb.

In the long night, the still night,
　　He kneels upon the sod;
And the brutal guards withhold
　　E'en the solemn Word of God!
In the long night, the still night,
　　He walks where Christ hath trod.

'Neath the blue morn, the sunny morn,
　　He dies upon the tree;
And he mourns that he can lose
　　But one life for Liberty;
And in the blue morn, the sunny morn,
　　His spirit wings are free.

But his last words, his message-words,
　　They burn, lest friendly eye
Should read how proud and calm
　　A patriot could die,
With his last words, his dying words,
　　A soldier's battle cry.

From the Fame-leaf and Angel-leaf,
    From monument and urn,
The sad of earth, the glad of heaven,
    His tragic fate shall learn;
But on Fame-leaf and Angel-leaf
    The name of HALE shall burn!

CARMEN BELLICOSUM

Guy Humphreys McMaster

In their ragged regimentals,
Stood the old Continentals,
    Yielding not,
While the grenadiers were lunging,
And like hail fell the plunging
    Cannon-shot;
        When the files
        Of the isles,
From the smoky night-encampment, bore the banner of the
                                        rampant

        Unicorn;
And grummer, grummer, grummer, rolled the roll of the
                                        drummer,

        Through the morn!

Then with eyes to the front all,
And with guns horizontal,
    Stood our sires;
And the balls whistled deadly,
And in streams flashing redly
    Blazed the fires
        As the roar
        On the shore,
Swept the strong battle-breakers o'er the green-sodded acres
        Of the plain;
And louder, louder, louder, cracked the black gunpowder,
        Cracking amain!

Now like smiths at their forges
Worked the red St. George's
    Cannoneers;
And the villainous saltpetre
Rung a fierce, discordant metre
    Round their ears:
        As the swift
        Storm-drift
With hot sweeping anger, came the horse-guards' clangor
        On our flanks.
Then higher, higher, higher, burned the old-fashioned fire
        Through the ranks!

Then the bare-headed colonel
Galloped through the white infernal
    Powder-cloud;
And his broadsword was swinging,
And his brazen throat was ringing
    Trumpet-loud.
        Then the blue
        Bullets flew,
And the trooper-jackets redden at the touch of the leaden
        Rifle-breath;
And rounder, rounder, rounder, roared the iron six-pounder,
        Hurling death!

MOLLY PITCHER

Kate Brownlee Sherwood

It was hurry and scurry at Monmouth town,
   For Lee was beating a wild retreat;
The British were riding the Yankee down,
   And panic was pressing on flying feet.

Galloping down like a hurricane
   Washington rode with his sword swung high,
Mighty as he of the Trojan plain
   Fired by a courage from the sky.

"Halt, and stand to your guns!" he cried.
   And a bombardier made swift reply.
Wheeling his cannon into the tide,
   He fell 'neath the shot of a foeman high.

Molly Pitcher sprang to his side,
   Fired as she saw her husband do.
Telling the king in his stubborn pride
   Women like men to their homes are true.

Washington rode from the bloody fray
   Up to the gun that a woman manned.
"Molly Pitcher, you saved the day,"
   He said, as he gave her a hero's hand.

He named her sergeant with manly praise,
   While her war-brown face was wet with tears—
A woman has ever a woman's ways,
   And the army was wild with cheers.

LAFAYETTE TO WASHINGTON
from *Valley Forge*

Maxwell Anderson

Lafayette to Washington:
      Shall I begin by saying
some things you know, but may have forgotten? This world
you have cut from the wilderness, is a new world, brighter
with sun in summer, colder with winter cold
than the world I knew. The air's strange-sharp, the voice
rings here with a hard ring. I find no man
but looks you in the eye and says his thought
in your teeth, and means it. This was not known before
on this star we inhabit. Europe has thirty kings
and a hundred million slaves. But here in this land
each man is a king and walks like a king, each woman
bears herself regally, like a queen. You will find
this is not easy to throw away. The air
of this coast has fired your blood and while three among
                                    you,
no more than three, hold hard against the old masters,
the kingdoms lessen and dwindle. They've felt your breath
and feared it, in the old world. Lose! now the gods
in heaven hear me, you cannot lose! Bow down
and humble yourselves if you can! It's not in you to bow
nor to speak humbly. It's a trick you've never learned
and cannot learn in this air!—As for these thrones
that men have bowed to, I've come from them lately and
                                  seen them,
how they're eaten down with old vices and slimed with
                                  worms
'til they crumble into moats! Lower your muzzles,
droop your flags! Even so the kingdoms falter
and go down of themselves!

LA FAYETTE

Dolly Madison

Born, nurtured, wedded, prized, within the pale
  Of peers and princes, high in camp—at court—
  He hears, in joyous youth, a wild report,
Swelling the murmurs of the Western gale,
Of a young people struggling to be free!
  Straight quitting all, across the wave he flies,
  Aids with his sword, wealth, blood, the high emprize!
And shares the glories of its victory.
  Then comes for fifty years a high romance
Of toils, reverses, sufferings, in the cause
  Of man and justice, liberty and France,
Crowned, at the last, with hope and wide applause.
Champion of Freedom! Well thy race was run!
All time shall hail thee, *Europe's noblest Son!*

CAPTAIN MOLLY

William Collins

On the bloody field of Monmouth
   Flashed the guns of Greene and Wayne,
Fiercely roared the tide of battle,
   Thick the sward was heaped with slain.
Foremost, facing death and danger,
   Hessian, horse, and grenadier,
In the vanguard, fiercely fighting,
   Stood an Irish Cannonier.

Loudly roared his iron cannon,
   Mingling ever in the strife,
And beside him, firm and daring,
   Stood his faithful Irish wife.
Of her bold contempt of danger
   Greene and Lee's Brigades could tell,
Every one knew "Captain Molly,"
   And the army loved her well.

Surged the roar of battle round them,
   Swiftly flew the iron hail,
Forward dashed a thousand bayonets,
   That lone battery to assail.
From the foeman's foremost columns
   Swept a furious fusillade,
Mowing down the massed battalions
   In the ranks of Greene's Brigade.

Fast and faster worked the gunner,
    Soiled with powder, blood, and dust,
English bayonets shone before him,
    Shot and shell around him burst;
Still he fought with reckless daring,
    Stood and manned her long and well,
Till at last the gallant fellow
    Dead—beside his cannon fell.

With a bitter cry of sorrow,
    And a dark and angry frown,
Looked that band of gallant patriots
    At their gunner stricken down.
"Fall back, comrades, it is folly
    Thus to strive against the foe."
"No! not so," cried Irish Molly;
    "We can strike another blow."

Quickly leaped she to the cannon,
    In her fallen husband's place,
Sponged and rammed it fast and steady,
    Fired it in the foeman's face.
Flashed another ringing volley,
    Roared another from the gun;
"Boys, hurrah!" cried gallant Molly,
    "For the flag of Washington."

Greene's Brigade, though shorn and shattered,
    Slain and bleeding half their men,
When they heard that Irish slogan,
    Turned and charged the foe again.
Knox and Wayne and Morgan rally,
    To the front they forward wheel,
And before their rushing onset
    Clinton's English columns reel.

Still the cannon's voice in anger
  Rolled and rattled o'er the plain,
Till there lay in swarms around it
  Mangled heaps of Hessian slain.
"Forward! charge them with the bayonet!"
  'Twas the voice of Washington,
And there burst a fiery greeting
  From the Irish woman's gun.

Monckton falls; against his columns
  Leap the troops of Wayne and Lee,
And before their reeking bayonets
  Clinton's red battalions flee.
Morgan's rifles, fiercely flashing,
  Thin the foe's retreating ranks,
And behind them onward dashing
  Ogden hovers on their flanks.

Fast they fly, these boasting Britons,
  Who in all their glory came,
With their brutal Hessian hirelings
  To wipe out our country's name.
Proudly floats the starry banner,
  Monmouth's glorious field is won,
And in triumph Irish Molly
  Stands beside her smoking gun.

TICONDEROGA

V. B. Wilson

The cold, gray light of the dawning
  On old Carillon falls,
And dim in the mist of the morning
  Stand the grim old fortress walls.
No sound disturbs the stillness
  Save the cataract's mellow roar,
Silent as death is the fortress,
  Silent the misty shore.

But up from the wakening waters
  Comes the cool, fresh morning breeze,
Lifting the banner of Britain,
  And whispering to the trees
Of the swift gliding boats on the waters
  That are nearing the fog-shrouded land,
With the old Green Mountain Lion,
  And his daring patriot band.

But the sentinel at the postern
  Heard not the whisper low;
He is dreaming of the banks of the Shannon
  As he walks on his beat to and fro,
Of the starry eyes in Green Erin
  That were dim when he marched away,
And a tear down his bronzed cheek courses,
  'T is the first for many a day.

A sound breaks the misty stillness,
   And quickly he glances around;
Through the mist, forms like towering giants
   Seem rising out of the ground;
A challenge, the firelock flashes,
   A sword cleaves the quivering air,
And the sentry lies dead by the postern,
   Blood staining his bright yellow hair.

Then, with a shout that awakens
   All the echoes of hillside and glen,
Through the low, frowning gate of the fortress,
   Sword in hand, rush the Green Mountain men.
The scarce wakened troops of the garrison
   Yield up their trust pale with fear;
And down comes the bright British banner,
   And out rings a Green Mountain cheer.

Flushed with pride, the whole eastern heavens
   With crimson and gold are ablaze;
And up springs the sun in his splendor
   And flings down his arrowy rays,
Bathing in sunlight the fortress,
   Turning to gold the grim walls,
While louder and clearer and higher
   Rings the song of the waterfalls.

Since the taking of Ticonderoga
   A century has rolled away;
But with pride the nation remembers
   That glorious morning in May.
And the cataract's silvery music
   Forever the story tells,
Of the capture of old Carillon,
   The chime of the silver bells.

EMILY GEIGER

Author Unknown

'Twas in the days of the Revolution,—
  Dark days were they and drear,—
And by Carolina firesides
  The women sat in fear;
For the men were away at the fighting,
  And sad was the news that came,
That the battle was lost; and the death-list
  Held many a loved one's name.

When as heart-sore they sat round the camp-fires,
  "What, ho! Who'll volunteer
To carry a message to Sumter?"
  A voice rang loud and clear.
There was a sudden silence,
  But not a man replied;
They knew too well of the peril
  Of one who dared that ride.

Outspoke then Emily Geiger
  With a rich flush on her cheek,—
"Give me the message to be sent;
  I am the one you seek.
For I am a Southern woman;
  And I'd rather do and dare
Than sit by a lonely fireside,
  My heart gnawed through with care."

They gave her the precious missive;
  And on her own good steed
She rode away, 'mid the cheers of the men,
  Upon her daring deed.
And away through the lonely forests,
  Steadily galloping on,
She saw the sun sink low in the sky,
  And in the west go down.

"Halt!—or I fire!" On a sudden
  A rifle clicked close by.
"Let you pass? Not we, till we know you are
  No messenger or spy."
"She's a Whig,—from her face,—I will wager,"
  Swore the officer of the day.
"To the guard-house, and send for a woman
  To search her without delay."

No time did she lose in bewailing;
  As the bolt creaked in the lock,
She quickly drew the precious note
  That was hidden in her frock.
And she read it through with hurried care,
  Then ate it piece by piece,
And calmly sat her down to wait
  Till time should bring release.

They brought her out in a little,
  And set her on her steed,
With many a rude apology,
  For his discourteous deed.
On, on, once more through the forest black,
  The good horse panting strains,
Till the sentry's challenge: "Who comes there?"
  Tells that the end she gains.

Ere an hour, in the camp of Sumter
  There was hurrying to and fro.
"Saddle and mount, saddle and mount,"
  The bugles shrilly blow.
"Forward trot!" and the long ranks wheel,
  And into the darkness glide:
Long shall the British rue that march
  And Emily Geiger's ride.

BETTY ZANE, September, 1777

Thomas Dunn English

A century since, out in the West,
A blockhouse was by Girty pressed—
Girty, the renegade, the dread
Of all that border, fiercely led
Five hundred Wyandots to gain
Plunder and scalp-locks from the slain;
And in this hold—Fort Henry then,
But Wheeling now—twelve boys and men
Guarded with watchful ward and care
Women and prattling children there,
Against their rude and savage foes,
And Betty Zane was one of those.

Now Betty's brothers and her sire
Were with her in this ring of fire,
And she was ready in her way,
To aid their labor day by day,
In all a quiet maiden might.
To mold the bullets for the fight,
And, quick to note and so report,
Watch every act outside the fort;
Or, peering through the loopholes, see
Each phase of savage strategy—
These were her tasks, and thus the maid
The toil-worn garrison could aid.

Still drearily the fight went on
Until a week had nearly gone,

When it was told—a whisper first,
And then in loud alarm it burst—
Their powder scarce was growing; they
Knew where a keg unopened lay
Outside the fort at Zane's—what now?
Their leader stood with anxious brow.
It must be had at any cost,
Or toil and fort and lives were lost.
Someone must do that work of fear;
What man of men would volunteer?

Two offered and so earnest they,
Neither his purpose would give way;
And Shepherd, who commanded, dare
Not pick or choose between the pair.
But ere they settled on the one
By whom the errand should be done,
Young Betty interposed and said,
"Let me essay the task instead.
Small matter 'twere if Betty Zane,
A useless woman should be slain;
But death, if death of one of those,
Gives too much vantage to our foes."

Her father smiled with pleasure grim—
Her pluck gave painful pride to him;
And while her brothers clamored "No"
He uttered "Boys, let Betty go!
She'll do it at less risk than you;
But keep her steady in your view,
And be your rifles shields for her.
If yonder foe make step or stir,
Pick off each wretch who draws a bead,
And so you'd serve her in her need.
Now I recover from surprise,
I think our Betty's purpose wise."

The gate was opened, on she sped;
The foe astonished, gazed, 'tis said,
And wondered at her purpose, till
She gained that log hut by the hill.
But when in apron wrapped the cask
She backward bore to close her task,
The foemen saw her aim at last
And poured their fire upon her fast.
Bullet on bullet near her fell,
While rang the Indians' angry yell;
But safely through that whirring rain,
Powder in arms, came Betty Zane.

A hundred years have passed since then;
The savage never came again.
Girty is dust; alike are dead
Those who assailed and those bestead.
Upon those half-cleared, rolling lands,
A crowded city proudly stands;
But of the many who reside
By green Ohio's rushing tide,
Not one has lineage prouder than
(Be he poor or rich) the man
Who boasts that in his spotless strain
Mingles the blood of Betty Zane.

JOHN PAUL JONES, September 23, 1779

Walt Whitman

Would you hear of an old-time sea fight?
Would you hear who won by the light of the moon and
        stars?
List to the yarn as my grandmother's father the sailor told it
        to me.

Our foe was no sulk in his ship I tell you (said he,)
His was the surly English pluck, and there is no tougher or
        truer, and never was, and never will be;
Along the lower'd eve he came horribly raking at us.
We closed with him, the yards entangled, the cannon
        touched.
My captain lashed fast with his own hands.

We had received some eighteen pound shots under the water,
On the lower gun deck two large pieces had burst at the
      first fire, killing all around and blowing up overhead.

Fighting at sundown, fighting at dark,
Ten o'clock at night, the full moon well up, our leaks on
        the gain, and five feet of water reported,
The master-at-arms loosing the prisoners confined in the
      after hold to give them a chance for themselves.

The transit to and from the magazine is now stopped by the
        sentinels,
They see so many strange faces they do not know whom to
        trust.

Our frigate takes fire,
The other asks if we demand quarter?
If our colors are struck and the fighting done?

Now I laugh content, for I hear the voice of my little
                                          captain,
We have not struck, he composedly cries, *we have just
                      begun our part of the fighting.*

Only three guns are in use,
One is directed by the captain himself against the enemy's
                                          mainmast,
Two well-serv'd with grape and canister silence his musketry
                            and clear his decks.

The tops alone second the fire of this little battery, especially
                                    the maintop,
They hold out bravely during the whole of the action.
Not a moment's cease,
The leaks gain fast on the pumps, the fire eats toward the
                            powder magazine.

One of the pumps has been shot away, it is generally
                      thought we are sinking.

Serene stands the little captain,
He is not hurried, his voice is neither high nor low,
His eyes give more light to us than our battle lanterns.

Toward twelve there in the beams of the moon they
                            surrender to us.

PAUL JONES

Author Unknown

An American frigate from Baltimore came,
Her guns mounted forty, the *Richard* by name;
Went to crisis in the channel of old England,
With a noble commander, Paul Jones was the man.

We had not sailed long before we did espy
A large forty-four, and a twenty close by:
These two warlike ships, full laden with store,
Our captain pursued to the bold Yorkshire shore.

At the hour of twelve, Pierre came alongside.
With a loud speaking-trumpet, "Whence came you?" he
                                                    cried;
"Quick give me an answer, I hailed you before,
Or this very instant a broadside I'll pour."

Paul Jones he exclaimed, "My brave boys, we'll not run:
Let every brave seaman stand close to his gun";
When a broadside was fired by these brave Englishmen,
We bold buckskin heroes returned it again.

We fought them five glasses, five glasses most hot,
Till fifty brave seamen lay dead on the spot,
And full seventy more lay bleeding in their gore,
Whilst Pierre's loud cannon on the *Richard* did roar.

Our gunner, affrighted, unto Paul Jones he came,
"Our ship is a-sinking, likewise in a flame,"

Paul Jones he replied, in the height of his pride,
"If we can do no better, we'll sink alongside."

At length our shot flew so quick, they could not stand;
The flag of proud Britain was forced to come down,
The *Alliance* bore down and the *Richard* did rake,
Which caused the heart of *Richard* to ache.

Come now, my brave buckskins, we've taken a prize,
A large forty-four, and a twenty likewise;
They are both noble vessels, well laden with store!
We will toss off the can to our country once more.

God help the poor widows, who shortly must weep
For the loss of their husbands, now sunk in the deep!
We'll drink to brave Paul Jones, who, with sword in hand,
Shone foremost in action, and gave us command.

TO THE MEMORY OF THE BRAVE AMERICANS

(under General Greene, in South Carolina, who fell in the action of September 8, 1781)

Philip Freneau

At Eutaw Springs the valiant died;
  Their limbs with dust are covered o'er—
Weep on, ye springs, your tearful tide;
  How many heroes are no more!

If in this wreck of ruin, they
  Can yet be thought to claim a tear,
O smite your gentle breast, and say
  The friends of freedom slumber here!

Thou, who shalt trace this bloody plain,
  If goodness rules thy generous breast,
Sigh for the wasted rural reign;
  Sigh for the shepherds, sunk to rest!

Stranger, their humble graves adorn;
  You too may fall, and ask a tear;
'Tis not the beauty of the morn
  That proves the evening shall be clear.—

They saw their injured country's woe;
  The flaming town, the wasted field;
Then rushed to meet the insulting foe;
  They took the spear—but left the shield.

Led by thy conquering genius, Greene,
  The Britons they compelled to fly;
None distant viewed the fatal plain,
  None grieved, in such a cause to die—

But, like the Parthian, famed of old,
  Who, flying, still their arrows threw,
These routed Britons, full as bold,
  Retreated, and retreating slew.

Now rest in peace, our patriot band;
  Though far from nature's limits thrown,
We trust they find a happier land,
  A brighter sunshine of their own.

ENGLAND AND AMERICA IN 1782

Alfred, Lord Tennyson

O thou, that sendest out the man
　To rule by land and sea,
Strong mother of a Lion-line,
Be proud of those strong sons of thine
　Who wrench'd their rights from thee!

What wonder if in noble heat
　Those men thine arms withstood,
Retaught the lesson thou had'st taught,
And in thy spirit with thee fought,—
　Who sprang from English blood!

But thou rejoice with liberal joy,
　Lift up thy rocky face,
And shatter, when the storms are black,
In many a streaming torrent black,
　The seas that shock thy base!

Whatever harmonies of law
　The growing world assume,
Thy work is thine—the single note
From that deep chord which Hampden smote
　Will vibrate to the doom.

WASHINGTON

George Gordon, Lord Byron

Where may the wearied eye repose
　When gazing on the Great;
Where neither guilty glory glows,
　Nor despicable state?
Yes—one—the first—the last—the best
The Cincinnatus of the West
　Whom envy dared not hate,
Bequeath the name of Washington
To make men blush there was but one!

OURS, AND ALL MEN'S

from *Under the Old Elm*

James Russell Lowell

Soldier and statesman, rarest unison,
High-poised example of great duties done
Simply as breathing, a world's honors worn
As life's indifferent gifts to all men born;
Dumb for himself, unless it were to God,
But for his barefoot soldier eloquent,
Tramping the snow to coral where they trod,
Held by his awe in hollow-eyed content;
Modest, yet firm as Nature's self; unblamed
Save by the men his nobler temper shamed;
Not honored then or now because he wooed
The popular voice, but that he still withstood;
Broadminded, higher-souled, there is but one
Who was all this and ours, and all men's—WASHINGTON.

GEORGE WASHINGTON

John Hall Ingham

This was the man God gave us when the hour
Proclaimed the dawn of Liberty begun;
Who dared a deed and died when it was done
Patient in triumph, temperate in power,—
Not striving like the Corsican to tower
To heaven, nor like great Philip's greater son
To win the world and weep for worlds unwon,
Or lose the star to revel in the flower.
The lives that serve the eternal verities
Alone do mold mankind. Pleasure and pride
Sparkle awhile and perish, as the spray
Smoking across the crests of cavernous seas
Is impotent to hasten or delay
The everlasting surges of the tide.

AT MOUNT VERNON

Thomas Curtis Clark

Along this path he walked, great Washington,
Who built a nation out of selfish men;
These trees he planted, here he stood and mused
On spring's first blossoms, or on autumn's gain.
By this loved river, flowing wide and free,
He sighed for rest from all the cares of state.
How dear his home! And yet he could not pause
While traitors tore his land with greed and hate;
He could not free himself, whose character
Was part and parcel of his country's name.
He found no lasting rest, though worn and spent,
Till death relieved him from the bonds of fame.
Through all the years, till freedom's day is run,
One name shall shine with splendor—WASHINGTON.

THE NAME OF WASHINGTON

Arthur Gordon Field

America, the land beloved,
  Today reveres the name of him
Whose character was free from guile,
  Whose fame the ages cannot dim.

They called him proud, but erred therein;
  No lord was he, though high of birth;
Though sprung from England's lofty peers,
  He served the lowliest of earth.

He turned his back on pride of name,
  On motherland and luxury,
To weld a horde of quarreling men
  Into a nation proudly free.

Wherever liberty is found,
  Wherever shines fair freedom's sun,
Men count America a friend
  And bless the name of Washington.

JOHN ADAMS

Rosemary and Stephen Vincent Benét

The old rutted roads have been turned to macadams,
But Quincy and Braintree remember the Adams.

There was John and John Quincy, Charles Francis and
                                                    Brooks
And Henry, who wrote most remarkable books.

And a number of others I will not describe,
But John—this is he—was the first of the tribe.

The son of a farmer, a lawyer by trade,
He was always on hand when our Nation was made.

A statesman of genius, a patriot of zeal,
He was vain as old Harry but true as cold steel.

He founded our Navy, from rudder to mast,
He saw that the bold Declaration was passed.

But he kept us from war with the French at a time
When to fight would have been little less than a crime.

For he wasn't hot-headed, though stubborn and fiery
And given to writing mean things in his diary.

He served but one term in the President's chair,
And his foes made it hot for him while he was there.

But, at eighty years old, he was still going strong
And convinced that no Adams could ever be wrong.

And his sons and his grandsons and all of his stock
Were chips of the selfsame, identical block.

Remarkable men, with the tart Adams quirk,
And the same Adams talent for doing good work

In spite of the tumult that always arose
When they carefully trod upon other folks' toes.

For their crotchets were theirs, but their virtues the
                                        Nation's,
And they served us superbly for four generations.

They could irritate Job, but they never were small.
—And this is John Adams who started them all.

BALLAD OF THE COMMON MAN

(For the Jefferson Memorial)

Alfred Kreymborg

To him who felt a human sea
Begin to rise for liberty,
  Build, O men, keep building!

To him who raised the human pen
That freed the first American,
  Build, O men, keep building!

For he is in the common star
Of all we live in, all we are
In sons and more sons near and far—
  Build, O men, keep building!

And rear your temple all around
Our common feet and common ground,
Giving our love a common sound—
  Build, O men, keep building!

And let us feel there is no night
Can ever hide the growing light—
The light he saw, the light he spread—
And all our sight, though he is dead—
  Build, O men, keep building!

And even though your labor's done
And the race may rest in Jefferson,
Rise up again, there's more to be done!
  Build, O men, keep building!
      Keep on building Men!

BATTLE-HYMN OF THE REPUBLIC

Julia Ward Howe

Mine eyes have seen the glory of the coming of the Lord:
He is trampling out the vintage where the grapes of wrath
are stored;
He hath loosed the fateful lightning of his terrible swift
sword:
His truth is marching on.

I have seen him in the watch-fires of a hundred circling
camps;
They have builded him an altar in the evening dews and
damps;
I can read his righteous sentence by the dim and flaring
lamps:
His day is marching on.

I have read a fiery gospel, writ in burnished rows of steel:
"As ye deal with my contemners, so with you my grace
shall deal;
Let the Hero, born of woman, crush the serpent with his
heel,
Since God is marching on."

He has sounded forth the trumpet that shall never call
retreat;
He is sifting out the hearts of men before his judgment-seat:
O, be swift, my soul, to answer him! be jubilant, my feet!
Our God is marching on.

In the beauty of the lilies Christ was born across the sea,
With a glory in his bosom that transfigures you and me;
As he died to make men holy, let us die to make men free,
    While God is marching on.

[A sixth stanza, as follows, was written by the author, but is seldom quoted.]

He is coming like the glory of the morning on the wave,
He is wisdom to the mighty, he is honor to the brave,
So the world shall be his footstool, and the soul of wrong
                                                    his slave,

    Our God is marching on!

AN ARMY CORPS ON THE MARCH

Walt Whitman

With its cloud of skirmishers in advance,
With now the sound of a single shot snapping like a whip,
        and now an irregular volley,
The swarming ranks press on and on, the dense brigades
             press on,
Glittering dimly, toiling under the sun—the dust-cover'd men,
In columns rise and fall to the undulations of the ground,
With artillery interspers'd—the wheels rumble, the horses
             sweat,
As the army corps advances.

BIVOUAC ON A MOUNTAIN SIDE

Walt Whitman

I see before me now a traveling army halting,
Below a fertile valley spread, with barns and the orchards
of summer,
Behind, the terraced sides of a mountain, abrupt, in places
rising high,
Broken, with rocks, with clinging cedars, with tall shapes
dingily seen,
The numerous camp-fires scatter'd near and far, some away
up on the mountain,
The shadowy forms of men and horses, looming, large-sized,
flickering,
And over all the sky—the sky! far, far out of reach,
studded, breaking out, the eternal stars.

SHILOH

A Requiem (April, 1862)

Herman Melville

Skimming lightly, wheeling still,
    The swallows fly low
Over the field in clouded days,
    The forest field of Shiloh—
Over the field where April rain
Solaced the parched one stretched in pain
Through the pause of night
That followed the Sunday fight
    Around the church of Shiloh—
The church so lone, the log-built one,
That echoed to many a parting groan
      And natural prayer
    Of dying foemen mingled there—
Foemen at morn, but friends at eve—
    Fame or country least their care:
(What like a bullet can undeceive!)
    But now they lie low,
While over them the swallows skim,
    And all is hushed at Shiloh.

BARBARA FRIETCHIE

John Greenleaf Whittier

Up from the meadows rich with corn,
Clear in the cool September morn,

The clustered spires of Frederick stand
Green-walled by the hills of Maryland.

Round about them orchards sweep,
Apple and peach tree fruited deep,

Fair as the garden of the Lord
To the eyes of the famished rebel horde,

On that pleasant morn of the early fall
When Lee marched over the mountain-wall;

Over the mountains winding down,
Horse and foot, into Frederick town.

Forty flags with their silver stars,
Forty flags with their crimson bars,

Flapped in the morning wind: the sun
Of noon looked down, and saw not one.

Up rose old Barbara Frietchie then,
Bowed with her fourscore years and ten;

Bravest of all in Frederick town,
She took up the flag the men hauled down;

In her attic window the staff she set,
To show that one heart was loyal yet.

Up the street came the rebel tread,
Stonewall Jackson riding ahead.

Under his slouched hat left and right
He glanced; the old flag met his sight.

"Halt!"—the dust-brown ranks stood fast.
"Fire!"—out blazed the rifle-blast.

It shivered the window, pane and sash;
It rent the banner with seam and gash.

Quick as it fell, from the broken staff
Dame Barbara snatched the silken scarf.

She leaned far out on the window-sill,
And shook it forth with a royal will.

"Shoot, if you must, this old gray head,
But spare your country's flag," she said.

A shade of sadness, a blush of shame,
Over the face of the leader came;

The nobler nature within him stirred
To life at that woman's deed and word;

"Who touches a hair on yon gray head
Dies like a dog! March on!" he said.

All day long through Frederick street
Sounded the tread of marching feet:

All day long that free flag tossed
Over the heads of the rebel host.

Ever its torn folds rose and fell
On the loyal winds that loved it well;

And through the hill-gaps sunset light
Shone over it with a warm good-night.

Barbara Frietchie's work is o'er,
And the Rebel rides on his raids no more.

Honor to her! and let a tear
Fall, for her sake, on Stonewall's bier.

Over Barbara Frietchie's grave,
Flag of Freedom and Union, wave!

Peace and order and beauty draw
Round thy symbol of light and law;

And ever the stars above look down
On thy stars below in Frederick town!

THE HIGH TIDE AT GETTYSBURG, July 3, 1863

Will Henry Thompson

A cloud possessed the hollow field,
The gathering battle's smoky shield:
  Athwart the gloom the lightning flashed,
  And through the cloud some horsemen dashed,
And from the heights the thunder pealed.

Then, at the brief command of Lee,
Moved out that matchless infantry,
  With Picket leading grandly down,
  To rush against the roaring crown.
Of those dread heights of destiny.

Far heard above the angry guns,
A cry across the tumult runs:
  The voice that rang through Shiloh's woods,
  And Chickamauga's solitudes:
The fierce South cheering on her sons!

Ah, how the withering tempest blew
Against the front of Pettigrew!
  A Khamsin wind that scorched and singed,
  Like that infernal flame that fringed
The British squares at Waterloo!

A thousand fell where Kemper led;
A thousand died where Garnett bled;

In blinding flame and strangling smoke
The remnant through the batteries broke,
And crossed the works with Armistead.

"Once more in glory's van with me!"
Virginia cried to Tennessee:
　"We two together, come what may,
　Shall stand upon those works today!"
The reddest day in history.

Brave Tennessee! In reckless way
Virginia heard her comrade say:
　"Close round this rent and riddle rag!"
　What time she set her battle flag
Amid the guns of Doubleday.

But who shall break the guards that wait
Before the awful face of Fate?
　The tattered standards of the South
　Were shriveled at the cannon's mouth,
And all her hopes were desolate.

In vain the Tennesseean set
His breast against the bayonet;
　In vain Virginia charged and raged,
　A tigress in her wrath uncaged,
Till all the hill was red and wet!

Above the bayonets, mixed and crossed,
Men saw a gray, gigantic ghost
　Receding through the battle cloud,
　And heard across the tempest loud
The death cry of a nation lost!

The brave went down! Without disgrace
They leaped to Ruin's red embrace;
    They only heard Fame's thunders wake,
    And saw the dazzling sunburst break
In smiles on Glory's bloody face!

They fell, who lifted up a hand
And bade the sun in heaven to stand;
    They smote and fell, who set the bars
    Against the progress of the stars,
And stayed the march of Motherland!

They stood, who saw the future come
On through the fight's delirium;
    They smote and stood, who held the hope
    Of nations on that slippery slope,
Amid the cheers of Christendom!

God lives! He forged the iron will
That clutched and held the trembling hill!
    God lives and reigns! He built and lent
    The heights for Freedom's battlement,
Where floats her flag in triumph still!

Fold up the banners! Smelt the guns!
Love rules. Her gentler purpose runs.
    A mighty mother turns in tears
    The pages of her battle years,
Lamenting all her fallen sons!

JOHN BURNS OF GETTYSBURG

Bret Harte

Have you heard the story that gossips tell
Of Burns of Gettysburg? No? Ah, well:
Brief is the story that hero earns,
Briefer the story of poor John Burns:
He was the fellow that won renown,—
The only man who didn't back down
When the rebels rode through his native town;
But held his own in the fight next day,
When all his townsfolk ran away.
That was in July, sixty-three,—
The very day that General Lee,
Flower of Southern chivalry,
Baffled and beaten, backward reeled
From a stubborn Meade and a barren field.

I might tell how, but the day before,
John Burns stood at his cottage door,
Looking down the village street,
Where, in the shade of his peaceful vine,
He heard the low of his gathered kine,
And felt their breath with incense sweet;
Or I might say, when the sunset burned
The old farm gable, he thought it turned
The milk that fell like a babbling flood
Into the milk-pail, red as blood!
Or how he fancied the hum of bees
Were bullets humming among the trees.

But all such fanciful thoughts as these
Were strange to a practical man like Burns,
Who minded only his own concerns,
Troubled no more by fancies fine
Than one of his calm-eyed, long-tailed kine,—
Quite old-fashioned and matter-of-fact,
Slow to argue, but quick to act.
That was the reason, as some folks say,
He fought so well on that terrible day.

And it was terrible. On the right
Raged for hours the heady fight,
Thundered the battery's double bass,—
Difficult music for men to face;
While on the left—where now the graves
Undulate like the living waves
That all that day unceasing swept
Up to the pits the rebels kept—
Round-shot ploughed the upland glades,
Sown with bullets, reaped with blades;
Shattered fences here and there
Tossed their splinters in the air;
The very trees were stripped and bare;
The barns that once held yellow grain
Were heaped with harvests of the slain;
The cattle bellowed on the plain,
The turkeys screamed with might and main,
The brooding barn-fowl left their rest
With strange shells bursting in each nest.

Just where the tide of battle turns,
Erect and lonely, stood old John Burns.
How do you think the man was dressed?
He wore an ancient long buff vest,
Yellow as saffron,—but his best;
And, buttoned over his manly breast,

Was a bright blue coat, with a rolling collar,
And large gilt buttons,—size of a dollar,—
With tails that the country folk called "swaller."
He wore a broad-brimmed, bell-crowned hat,
White as the locks on which it sat.
Never had such a sight been seen
For forty years on the village green,
Since old John Burns was a country beau,
And went to the "quiltings" long ago.

Close at his elbows all that day,
Veterans of the Peninsula,
Sunburnt and bearded, charged away;
And striplings, downy of lip and chin,—
Clerks that the Home-Guard mustered in,—
Glanced, as they passed, at the hat he wore,
Then at the rifle his right hand bore;
And hailed him, from out their youthful lore,
With scraps of slangy repertoire:
"How are you, White Hat?" "Put her through!"
"Your head's level!" and "Bully for you!"
Called him "Daddy,"—begged he'd disclose
The name of the tailor who made his clothes,
And what was the value he set on those;
While Burns, unmindful of jeer or scoff,
Stood there picking the rebels off,—
With his long brown rifle, and bell-crowned hat,
And the swallow-tails they were laughing at.

'Twas but a moment, for that respect
Which clothes all courage their voices checked;
And something the wildest could understand
Spake in the old man's strong right hand,
And his corded throat, and the lurking frown
Of his eyebrows under his old bell-crown;
Until, as they gazed, there crept an awe

Through the ranks in whispers, and some men saw,
In the antique vestments and long white hair,
The Past of the Nation in battle there;
And some of the soldiers since declare
That the gleam of his old white hair afar,
Like the crested plume of the brave Navarre,
That day was their oriflamme of war.

So raged the battle. You know the rest:
How the rebels, beaten and backward pressed,
Broke at the final charge and ran.
At which John Burns—a practical man—
Shouldered his rifle, unbent his brows,
And then went back to his bees and cows.
That is the story of old John Burns;
This is the moral the reader learns:
In fighting the battle, the question's whether
You'll show a hat that's white, or a feather!

WE'RE TENTING TO-NIGHT

Walter Kittredge

We're tenting to-night on the old camp-ground,
  Give us a song to cheer
Our weary hearts, a song of home
  And friends we love so dear.
Many are the hearts that are weary to-night,
  Wishing for the war to cease;
Many are the hearts looking for the right,
  To see the dawn of peace.
Tenting to-night, tenting to-night,
  Tenting on the old camp-ground.

We've been tenting to-night on the old camp-ground,
  Thinking of days gone by,
Of the loved ones at home that gave us the hand,
  And the tear that said "good-bye"!
Many are the hearts that are weary to-night, etc.

We are weary of war on the old camp-ground,
  Many are the dead and gone
Of the brave and true who have left their homes,
  Others wounded long.
Many are the hearts that are weary to-night, etc.

We've been fighting to-day on the old camp-ground,
  Many are lying near;
Some are dead—and dying are some,
  Many a one in tears.
Many are the hearts that are weary to-night,
  To see the dawn of peace.
Dying to-night, dying to-night,
  Dying on the old camp-ground.

WHEN JOHNNY COMES MARCHING HOME

Patrick Sarsfield Gilmore

When Johnny comes marching home again,
   Hurrah! hurrah!
We'll give him a hearty welcome then,
   Hurrah! hurrah!
The men will cheer, and the boys will shout,
The ladies, they will all turn out,
   And we'll all feel gay,
When Johnny comes marching home.

The old church-bell will peal with joy,
   Hurrah! hurrah!
To welcome home our darling boy,
   Hurrah! hurrah!
The village lads and lasses say,
With roses they will strew the way;
   And we'll all feel gay,
When Johnny comes marching home.

Get ready for the jubilee,
   Hurrah! hurrah!
We'll give the hero three times three,
   Hurrah! hurrah!
The laurel-wreath is ready now
To place upon his loyal brow,
   And we'll all feel gay,
When Johnny comes marching home.

Let love and friendship on that day,
　　Hurrah! hurrah!
Their choicest treasures then display,
　　Hurrah! hurrah!
And let each one perform some part,
To fill with joy the warrior's heart;
　　And we'll all feel gay,
When Johnny comes marching home.

THE BLUE AND THE GRAY

Francis Miles Finch

By the flow of the inland river,
  Whence the fleets of iron have fled,
Where the blades of the grave grass quiver,
  Asleep are the ranks of the dead;—
    Under the sod and the dew,
      Waiting the judgment day;—
    Under the one, the Blue;
      Under the other, the Gray.

These in the robings of glory,
  Those in the gloom of defeat,
All with the battle blood gory,
  In the dusk of eternity meet;—
    Under the sod and the dew,
      Waiting the judgment day;—
    Under the laurel, the Blue;
      Under the willow, the Gray.

From the silence of sorrowful hours
  The desolate mourners go,
Lovingly laden with flowers
  Alike for the friend and the foe,—
    Under the sod and the dew,
      Waiting the judgment day;—
    Under the roses, the Blue;
      Under the lilies, the Gray.

So with an equal splendor
  The morning sun rays fall,
With a touch, impartially tender,
  On the blossoms blooming for all;—
    Under the sod and the dew,
      Waiting the judgment day;—
    'Broidered with gold, the Blue;
      Mellowed with gold, the Gray.

So, when the summer calleth,
  On forest and field of grain
With an equal murmur falleth
  The cooling drip of the rain;—
    Under the sod and the dew,
      Waiting the judgment day;—
    Wet with the rain, the Blue;
      Wet with the rain, the Gray.

Sadly, but not with upbraiding,
  The generous deed was done;
In the storm of the years that are fading,
  No braver battle was won;—
    Under the sod and the dew,
      Waiting the judgment day;—
    Under the blossoms, the Blue;
      Under the garlands, the Gray.

No more shall the war cry sever,
  Or the winding rivers be red;
They banish our anger forever
  When they laurel the graves of our dead!
    Under the sod and the dew,
      Waiting the judgment day;—
    Love and tears for the Blue,
      Tears and love for the Gray.

ODE TO THE CONFEDERATE DEAD IN MAGNOLIA CEMETERY

Henry Timrod

Sleep sweetly in your humble graves,
 Sleep, martyrs of a fallen cause;
Though yet no marble column craves
 The pilgrim here to pause.

In seeds of laurel in the earth
 The blossom of your fame is blown,
And somewhere, waiting for its birth,
 The shaft is in the stone!

Meanwhile, behalf the tardy years
 Which keep in trust your storied tombs,
Behold! your sisters bring their tears,
 And these memorial blooms.

Small tributes! but your shades will smile
 More proudly on these wreaths today,
Than when some cannon-moulded pile
 Shall overlook this bay.

Stoop, angels, hither from the skies!
 There is no holier spot of ground
Than where defeated valor lies,
 By mourning beauty crowned!

O CAPTAIN! MY CAPTAIN!

Walt Whitman

O Captain! my Captain! our fearful trip is done,
The ship has weathered every rack, the prize we sought is
                                                        won,
The port is near, the bells I hear, the people all exulting,
While follow eyes the steady keel, the vessel grim and daring
   But O heart! heart! heart!
    O the bleeding drops of red,
   Where on the deck my Captain lies,
    Fallen cold and dead.

O Captain! my Captain! rise up and hear the bells;
Rise up—for you the flag is flung—for you the bugle trills,
For you bouquets and ribboned wreaths—for you the
                                                shores a-crowding,
For you they call, the swaying mass, their eager faces
                                                        turning;
   Here Captain! dear father!
    This arm beneath your head!
   It is some dream that on the deck
    You've fallen cold and dead.

My Captain does not answer, his lips are pale and still,
My father does not feel my arm, he has no pulse nor will,
The ship is anchored safe and sound, its voyage closed and
                                                        done,
From fearful trip the victor ship comes in with object won;
Exult O shores, and ring O bells!
   But I with mournful tread,
Walk the deck my Captain lies,
    Fallen cold and dead.

LINCOLN, THE MAN OF THE PEOPLE

Edwin Markham

When the Norn Mother saw the Whirlwind Hour
Greatening and darkening as it hurried on,
She left the Heaven of Heroes and came down
To make a man to meet the mortal need.
She took the tired clay of the common road—
Clay warm yet with the genial heat of earth,
Dashed through it all a strain of prophecy;
Tempered the heap with thrill of human tears;
Then mixed a laughter with the serious stuff.
Into the shape she breathed a flame to light
That tender, tragic, ever-changing face;
And laid on him a sense of the Mystic Powers,
Moving—all hushed—behind the mortal veil.
Here was a man to hold against the world,
A man to match the mountains and the sea.

The color of the ground was in him, the red earth;
The smack and tang of elemental things:
The rectitude and patience of the cliff;
The good will of the rain that loves all leaves;
The friendly welcome of the wayside well;
The courage of the bird that dares the sea;
The gladness of the wind that shakes the corn;
The pity of the snow that hides all scars;
The secrecy of streams that make their way
Under the mountain to the rifted rock;
The tolerance and equity of light
That gives as freely to the shrinking flower
As to the great oak flaring to the wind—

To the grave's low hill as to the Matterhorn
That shoulders out the sky. Sprung from the West,
He drank the valorous youth of a new world.
The strength of virgin forests braced his mind,
The hush of spacious prairies stilled his soul.
His words were oaks in acorns; and his thoughts
Were roots that firmly gripped the granite truth.

Up from the log cabin to the Capitol,
One fire was on his spirit, one resolve—
To send the keen ax to the root of wrong,
Clearing a free way for the feet of God,
The eyes of conscience testing every stroke,
To make his deed the measure of a man.
He built the rail pile as he built the State,
Pouring his splendid strength through every blow;
The grip that swung the ax in Illinois
Was on the pen that set the people free.

So came the Captain with the mighty heart,
And when the judgment thunders split the house,
Wrenching the rafters from their ancient rest,
He held the ridgepole up, and spiked again
The rafters of the Home. He held his place—
Held the long purpose like a growing tree—
Held on through blame and faltered not at praise.
And when he fell in whirlwind, he went down
As when a lordly cedar, green with boughs,
Goes down with a great shout upon the hills,
And leaves a lonely place against the sky.

THERE WAS A DARKNESS IN
THIS MAN

from *Lincoln*

John Gould Fletcher

There was a darkness in this man; an immense and hollow
                                                    darkness,
Of which we may not speak, nor share with him, nor enter;
A darkness through which strong roots stretched downwards
                                                into the earth
Towards old things;
Towards the herdman-kings who walked the earth and
                                            spoke with God,
Towards the wanderers who sought for they knew not
                        what, and found their goal at last;
Towards the men who waited, only waited patiently when
                                            all seemed lost,
Many bitter winters of defeat;
Down to the granite of patience
These roots swept, knotted fibrous roots, prying, piercing,
                                                    seeking,
And drew from the living rock and the living waters about it
The red sap to carry upwards to the sun.

Not proud, but humble,
Only to serve and pass on, to endure to the end through
                                                    service;
For the ax is laid at the root of the trees, and all that
                            bring not forth good fruit
Shall be cut down on the day to come and cast into the fire.

There is silence abroad in the land today,
And in the hearts of men, a deep and anxious silence;
And, because we are still at last, those bronze lips slowly
                                                        open,

Those hollow and weary eyes take on a gleam of light.

The clamor of cannon dies down, the furnace-mouth of the
battle is silent.
The midwinter sun dips and descends, the earth takes on
afresh its bright colors.

But he whom we mocked and obeyed not, he whom we
scorned and mistrusted,
He has descended, like a god, to his rest.

Over the uproar of cities,
Over the million intricate threads of life wavering and
crossing,
In the midst of problems we know not, tangling, perplexing,
ensnaring,
Rises one white tomb alone.
Beam over it, stars.
Wrap it round, stripes—stripes red for the pain that he bore
for you—
Enfold it forever, O flag, rent, soiled, but repaired through
your anguish;
Long as you keep him there safe, the nations shall bow to
your law.

Strew over him flowers:
Blue forget-me-nots from the north, and the bright pink
arbutus
From the east, and from the west rich orange blossoms,
But from the heart of the land take the passionflower;
Rayed, violet, dim,
With the nails that pierced, the cross that he bore and the
circlet,
And beside it there lay also one lonely snow-white magnolia,
Bitter for remembrance of the healing which has passed.

ABRAHAM LINCOLN

Mildred Meigs

Remember he was poor and country-bred;
His face was lined; he walked with awkward gait.
Smart people laughed at him sometimes and said,
"How can so very plain a man be great?"

Remember he was humble, used to toil.
Strong arms he had to build a shack, a fence,
Long legs to tramp the woods, to plow the soil,
A head chuck full of backwoods common sense.

Remember all he ever had he earned,
He walked in time through stately White House doors;
But all he knew of men and life he learned
In little backwoods cabins, country stores.

Remember that his eyes could light with fun;
That wisdom, courage, set his name apart;
But when the rest is duly said and done,
Remember that men loved him for his heart.

WHEN LILACS LAST IN THE DOORYARD BLOOM'D

Walt Whitman

I

When lilacs last in the dooryard bloom'd,
And the great star early droop'd in the western sky in the
night,
I mourn'd, and yet shall mourn with ever-returning spring.
Ever-returning spring, trinity sure to me you bring,
Lilac blooming perennial and drooping star in the west,
And thought of him I love.

II

O powerful western fallen star!
O shades of night—O moody, tearful night!
O great star disappear'd—O the black murk that hides the
star!
O cruel hands that hold me powerless—O helpless soul of me!
O harsh surrounding cloud that will not free my soul.

III

In the dooryard fronting an old farm-house near the
white-wash'd palings,
Stands the lilac-bush tall-growing with heart-shaped leaves of
rich green,
With many a pointed blossom rising delicate, with the
perfume strong I love.
With every leaf a miracle—and from this bush in the
dooryard,

With delicate-color'd blossoms and heart-shaped leaves of rich
green,

A sprig with its flower I break.

IV

In the swamp in secluded recesses,
A shy and hidden bird is warbling a song.
Solitary the thrush,
The hermit withdrawn to himself, avoiding the settlements,
Sings by himself a song.
Song of the bleeding throat,
Death's outlet song of life (for well dear brother I know,
If thou wast not granted to sing thou would'st surely die).

V

Over the breast of the spring, the land, amid cities,
Amid lanes and through old woods, where lately the violets
peep'd from the ground, spotting the gray debris,
Amid the grass in the fields each side of the lanes, passing
the endless grass,
Passing the yellow-spear'd wheat, every grain from its shroud
in the dark-brown fields uprisen,
Passing the apple-tree blows of white and pink in the
orchards,
Carrying a corpse to where it shall rest in the grave,
Night and day journeys a coffin.

VI

Coffin that passes through lanes and streets,
Through day and night with the great cloud darkening the
land,
With the pomp of the inloop'd flags with the cities draped
in black,

With the show of the States themselves as of crape-veil'd
women standing,
With processions long and winding and the flambeaus of the
night,
With the countless torches lit, with the silent sea of faces
and the unbared heads,
With the waiting depot, the arriving coffin, and the sombre
faces,
With dirges through the night, with the thousand voices
rising strong and solemn,
With all the mournful voices of the dirges pour'd around the
coffin,
The dim-lit churches and the shuddering organs—where amid
these you journey,
With the tolling tolling bells' perpetual clang,
Here, coffin that slowly passes,
I give you my sprig of lilac.

VII

(Nor for you, for one alone,
Blossoms and branches green to coffins all I bring,
For fresh as the morning, thus would I chant a song for you
O sane and sacred death.

All over bouquets of roses,
O death, I cover you over with roses and early lilies,
But mostly and now the lilac that blooms the first,
Copious I break, I break the sprigs from the bushes,
With loaded arms I come, pouring for you,
For you and the coffins all of you O death.)

VIII

O western orb sailing the heaven,
Now I know what you must have meant as a month since I
walk'd,

As I walk'd in silence the transparent shadowy night,
As I saw you had something to tell as you bent to me night
after night,
As you droop'd from the sky low down as if to my side
(while the other stars all look'd on),
As we wander'd together the solemn night (for something I
know not what kept me from sleep),
As the night advanced, and I saw on the rim of the west
how full you were of woe,
As I stood on the rising ground in the breeze in the cool
transparent night,
As I watch'd where you pass'd and was lost in the
netherward black of the night,
As my soul in its trouble dissatisfied sank, as where you sad
orb,
Concluded, dropt in the night, and was gone.

IX

Sing on there in the swamp,
O singer bashful and tender, I hear your notes, I hear your
call,
I hear, I come presently, I understand you,
But a moment I linger, for the lustrous star has detain'd me,
The star my departing comrade holds and detains me.

X

O how shall I warble myself for the dead one there I loved?
And how shall I deck my song for the large sweet soul
that has gone?
And what shall my perfume be for the grave of him I love?

Sea-winds blown from east and west,
Blown from the Eastern sea and blown from the Western
sea, till there on the prairies meeting,

These and with these and the breath of my chant,
I'll perfume the grave of him I love.

XI

O what shall I hang on the chamber walls?
And what shall the pictures be that I hang on the walls,
To adorn the burial-house of him I love?

Pictures of growing spring and farms and homes,
With the Fourth-month eve at sundown and the gray smoke
                                        lucid and bright,
With floods of the yellow gold of the gorgeous, indolent,
                        sinking sun, burning, expanding the air,
With the fresh sweet herbage under foot, and the pale green
                            leaves of the trees prolific,
In the distance the flowering glaze, the breast of the river,
                        with a wind-dapple here and there,
With ranging hills on the banks, with many a line against
                                the sky, and shadows,
And the city at hand with dwellings so dense, and stacks of
                                            chimneys,
And all the scenes of life and the workshops, and the
                        workmen homeward returning.

XII

Lo, body and soul—this land,
My own Manhattan with spires, and the sparkling and
                            hurrying tides, and the ships,
The varied and ample land, the South and the North in the
                    light, Ohio's shores and flashing Missouri,
And ever the far-spreading prairies cover'd with grass and
                                                corn.

Lo, the most excellent sun so calm and haughty,
The violet and purple morn with just-felt breezes,

The gentle soft-born measureless light,
The miracle spreading bathing all, the fulfill'd noon,
The coming eve delicious, the welcome night and the stars,
Over my cities shining all, enveloping man and land.

XIII

Sing on, sing on you gray-brown bird,
Sing from the swamps, the recesses, pour your chant from
the bushes,
Limitless out of the dusk, out of the cedars and pines.

Sing on dearest brother, warble your reedy song,
Loud human song, with voice of uttermost woe.

O liquid and free and tender!
O wild and loose to my soul—O wondrous singer!
You only I hear—yet the star holds me (but will soon
depart),
Yet the lilac with mastering odor holds me.

XIV

Now while I sat in the day and look'd forth,
In the close of the day with its light and the fields of
spring, and the farmers preparing their crops,
In the large unconscious scenery of my land with its lakes
and forests,
In the heavenly aerial beauty (after the perturb'd winds and
the storms),
Under the arching heavens of the afternoon swift passing,
and the voices of children and women,
The many-moving sea-tides, and I saw the ships how they
sail'd,
And the summer approaching with richness, and the fields all
busy with labor,

And the infinite separate houses, how they all went on,
    each with its meals and minutia of daily usages,
And the streets how their throbbings throbb'd, and the cities
                pent--low, then and there,
Falling upon them all and among the mall, enveloping me
                with the rest,
Appear'd the cloud, appear'd the long black trail,
And I knew death, its thought, and the sacred knowledge of
                death.

Then with the knowledge of death as walking one side of me.

And the thought of death close-walking the other side of me,
And I in the middle as with companions, and as holding the
                hands of companions,
I fled forth to the hiding receiving night that talks not.
Down to the shores of the water, the path by the swamp in
                the dimness,
To the solemn shadowy cedars and ghostly pines so still.

And the singer so shy to the rest receiv'd me,
The gray-brown bird I know receiv'd us comrades three,
And he sang the carol of death, and a verse for him I love.

From deep secluded recesses,
From the fragrant cedars and the ghostly pines so still,
Came the carol of the bird.

And the charm of the carol rapt me,
As I held as if by their hands my comrades in the night,
And the voice of my spirit tallied the song of the bird.

Come lovely and soothing death,
Undulate round the world, serenely arriving, arriving,
In the day, in the night, to all, to each,
Sooner or later delicate death.

Prais'd be the fathomless universe,
For life and joy, and for objects and knowledge curious,
And for love, sweet love—but praise! praise! praise!
For the sure-enwinding arms of cool-enfolding death.

Dark mother always gliding near with soft feet,
Have none chanted for thee a chant of fullest welcome?
Then I chant it for thee, I glorify thee above all,
I bring thee a song that when thou must indeed come, come
                                           unfalteringly.

Approach strong deliveress,
When it is so, when thou hast taken them I joyously sing
                                   the dead,
Lost in the loving floating ocean of thee,
Laved in the flood of thy bliss O death.

From me to thee glad serenades,
Dances for thee I propose saluting thee, adornments and
                                feastings for thee,
And the sights of the open landscape and the high-spread sky
                                are fitting,
And life and the fields, and the huge and thoughtful night.

The night in silence under many a star,
The ocean shore and the husky whispering wave whose
                                 voice I know,
And the soul turning to thee O vast and well-veil'd death,
And the body gratefully nestling close to thee.

Over the tree-tops I float thee a song,
Over the rising and sinking waves, over the myriad fields and
                                the prairies wide,
Over the dense-pack'd cities all and the teeming wharves and
                                ways,
I float this carol with joy, with joy to thee O death.

XV

To the tally of my soul,
Loud and strong kept up the gray-brown bird,
With pure deliberate notes spreading, filling the night.

Loud in the pines and cedars dim,
Clear in the freshness moist and the swamp-perfume,
And I with my comrades there in the night.

While my sight that was bound in my eyes unclosed,
As to long panoramas of visions.

And I saw askant the armies,
I saw as in noiseless dreams hundreds of battle-flags,
Borne through the smoke of the battles and pierc'd with
                              missiles I saw them,
And carried hither and yon through the smoke, and torn and
                              bloody,
And at last but a few shreds left on the staffs (and all in
                              silence),
And the staffs all splinter'd and broken.

I saw battle-corpses, myriads of them,
And the white skeletons of young men, I saw them,
I saw the debris and debris of all the slain soldiers of the
                              war,
But I saw they were not as was thought,
They themselves were fully at rest, they suffer'd not,
The living remain'd and suffer'd, the mother suffer'd,
And the wife and the child and the musing comrade suffer'd,
And the armies that remain'd suffer'd.

XVI

Passing the visions, passing the night,
Passing, unloosing the hold of my comrades' hands,

Passing the song of the hermit bird and the tallying song of
my soul,
Victorious song, death's outlet song, yet varying ever-altering
song,
As low and wailing, yet clear the notes, rising and falling,
flooding the night,
Sadly sinking and fainting, as warning and warning, and yet
again bursting with joy,
Covering the earth and filling the spread of the heaven,
As that powerful psalm in the night I heard from recesses,
Passing, I leave thee lilac with heart-shaped leaves,
I leave thee there in the dooryard, blooming, returning with
spring.

I cease from my song for thee,
From my gaze on thee in the west, fronting the west,
communing with thee,
O comrade lustrous with silver face in the night.

Yet each to keep and all, retrievements out of the night,
The song, the wondrous chant of the gray-brown bird,
And the tallying chant, the echo arous'd in my soul,
With the lustrous and drooping star with the countenance
full of woe,
With the holders holding my hand nearing the call of the
bird,
Comrades mine and I in the midst, and their memory ever to
keep, for the dead I loved so well,
For the sweetest, wisest soul of all my days and lands—and
this for his dear sake,
Lilac and star and bird twined with the chant of my soul,
There in the fragrant pines and the cedars dusk and dim.

ABRAHAM LINCOLN WALKS
AT MIDNIGHT

(*in Springfield, Illinois*)

Vachel Lindsay

It is portentous, and a thing of state
That here at midnight, in our little town
A mourning figure walks, and will not rest,
Near the old court-house pacing up and down,

Or by his homestead, or in shadowed yards
He lingers where his children used to play,
Or through the market, on the well-worn stones
He stalks until the dawn-stars burn away.

A bronzed, lank man! His suit of ancient black,
A famous high top-hat and plain worn shawl
Make him the quaint great figure that men love,
The prairie-lawyer, master of us all.

He cannot sleep upon his hillside now.
He is among us:—as in times before!
And we who toss and lie awake for long
Breathe deep, and start, to see him pass the door.

His head is bowed. He thinks on men and kings.
Yes, when the sick world cries, how can he sleep?
Too many peasants fight, they know not why,
Too many homesteads in black terror weep.

The sins of all the war-lords burn his heart.
He sees the dreadnaughts scouring every main.

He carries on his shawl-wrapped shoulders now
The bitterness, the folly and the pain.

He cannot rest until a spirit-dawn
Shall come;—the shining hope of Europe free:
The league of sober folk, the Workers' Earth,
Bringing long peace to Cornland, Alp and Sea.

It breaks his heart that kings must murder still,
That all his hours of travail here for men
Seem yet in vain. And who will bring white peace
That he may sleep upon his hill again?

I AM THE FLAG

Lawrence M. Jones

I am a composite being of all the people of America.
I am the union if you are united.
I am one and indivisible if you are undivided.
I am as strong as the weakest link.
I am an emblem of your country.
I am a symbol of a shadow of the real.
I am a sign pointing to past achievements.
I am a promise of greater things for the future.
I am what you make me.
I am purity if you are pure.
I am bravery if you are brave.
I am loyalty if you are loyal.

I am honor if you are honorable.
I am goodness if you are good.
I am hope if you are hopeful.
I am truth if you are true.

I am the Constitution.
I am law and order.
I am tolerance or intolerance as you force me to be.
I am liberty as you understand liberty.
I am as a pillar of fire by night, but you must provide the
fuel.

I march at the head of the column, but you must carry me
on.

I stand for greater and more glorious achievement than can
be found in recorded history, but you must be my
inspiration.
I AM THE FLAG.

I HEAR AMERICA SINGING

Walt Whitman

I hear America singing, the varied carols I hear:
Those of mechanics—each one singing his, as it should be,
                     blithe and strong;
The carpenter singing his, as he measures his plank or beam,
The mason singing his, as he makes ready for work, or
                     leaves off work;
The boatman singing what belongs to him in his boat—the
               deckhand singing on the steamboat deck;
The shoemaker singing as he sits on his bench—the hatter
                     singing as he stands;
The wood cutter's song—the ploughboy's on his way in the
           morning, or at noon intermission, or at sundown;
The delicious singing of the mother—or of the young wife
              at work—or of the girl sewing or washing—
Each singing what belongs to him or her and to none else;
The day what belongs to the day—at night, the party of
                    young fellows, robust, friendly,
Singing, with open mouths, their strong melodious songs.

AMERICA GREETS AN ALIEN

Author Unknown

Hail, guest! We ask not what thou art.
If friend, we greet thee hand and heart;
If stranger, such no longer be;
If foe, our love shall conquer thee.

THE NEW COLOSSUS

Emma Lazarus

Not like the brazen giant of Greek fame,
With conquering limbs astride from land to land;
Here at our sea-washed, sunset gates shall stand
A mighty woman with a torch, whose flame
Is the imprisoned lightning, and her name
Mother of Exiles. From her beacon-hand
Glows world-wide welcome; her mild eyes command
The air-bridged harbor that twin cities frame.
"Keep, ancient lands, your storied pomp!" cries she
With silent lips. "Give me your tired, your poor,
Your huddled masses yearning to breathe free,
The wretched refuse of your teeming shore.
Send these, the homeless, tempest-tost to me,
I lift my lamp beside the golden door!"

THE POOR VOTER ON ELECTION DAY

John Greenleaf Whittier

The proudest now is but my peer,
    The highest not more high;
Today, of all the weary year,
    A king of men am I.
Today, alike are great and small,
    The nameless and the known;
My palace is the people's hall,
    The ballot-box my throne!

Who serves today upon the list
    Beside the served shall stand;
Alike the brown and wrinkled fist,
    The gloved and dainty hand!
The rich is level with the poor,
    The weak is strong today;
And sleekest broadcloth counts no more
    Than homespun frock of gray.

Today let pomp and vain pretense
    My stubborn right abide;
I set a plain man's common sense
    Against the pedant's pride.
Today shall simple manhood try
    The strength of gold and land;
The wide world has not wealth to buy
    The power in my right hand!

While there's a grief to seek redress,
    Or balance to adjust,
Where weighs our living manhood less
    Than Mammon's vilest dust—
While there's a right to need my vote,
    A wrong to sweep away,
Up! clouted knee and ragged coat!
    A man's a man today!

I AM AN AMERICAN

Elias Lieberman

I am an American.
My father belongs to the Sons of the Revolution;
My mother, to the Colonial Dames.
One of my ancestors pitched tea overboard in Boston
                                                    Harbor;
Another stood his ground with Warren;
Another hungered with Washington at Valley Forge.
My forefathers were America in the making:
They spoke in her council halls;
They died on her battle-fields;
They commanded her ships;
They cleared her forests.
Dawns reddened and paled.
Stanch hearts of mine beat fast at each new star
In the nation's flag.
Keen eyes of mine foresaw her greater glory:
The sweep of her seas.
The plenty of her plains.
The man-hives in her billion-wired cities.
Every drop of blood in me holds a heritage of patriotism.
I am proud of my past.
I am an American.

I am an American.
My father was an atom of dust,
My mother a straw in the wind,
To His Serene Majesty.
One of my ancestors died in the mines of Siberia;

Another was crippled for life by twenty blows of the knout;
Another was killed defending his home during the massacres.
The history of my ancestors is a trail of blood
To the palace-gate of the Great White Czar.
But then the dream came—
The dream of America.
In the light of the Liberty torch
The atom of the dust became a man
And the straw in the wind became a woman
For the first time.
"See," said my father, pointing to the flag that fluttered near,
"The flag of stars and stripes is yours;
It is the emblem of the promised land.
It means, my son, the hope of humanity.
Live for it—die for it!"
Under the open sky of my new county I swore to do so;
And every drop of blood in me will keep that vow.
I am proud of my future.
I am an American.

AMERICA WAS SCHOOLMASTERS

Robert P. Tristram Coffin

America was forests,
America was grain,
Wheat from dawn to sunset,
And rainbows trailing rain.

America was beavers,
Buffalo in seas,
Cornsilk and the johnnycake,
Songs of scythes and bees.

America was brown men
With eyes full of the sun,
But America was schoolmasters,
Tall one by lonely one.

They hewed oak, carried water,
Their hands were knuckleboned,
They piled on loads of syntax
Till the small boys groaned.

They taught the girls such manners
As stiffened them for life,
But made many a fine speller,
Good mother and good wife.

They took small wiry children,
Wild as panther-cats,

And turned them into reasoning,
Sunny democrats.

They caught a nation eager,
They caught a nation young,
They taught the nation fairness,
Thrift, and the golden tongue.

They started at the bottom
And built up strong and sweet,
They shaped our minds and morals
With switches on the seat!

COOL TOMBS

Carl Sandburg

When Abraham Lincoln was shoveled into the tombs,
   he forgot the copperheads and the assassin . . . in
   the dust, in the cool tombs.

And Ulysses Grant lost all thought of con men and Wall
   Street, cash and collateral turned ashes . . . in the
   dust, in the cool tombs.

Pocahontas' body, lovely as a poplar, sweet as a red haw
   in November or a pawpaw in May, did she wonder?
   does she remember? . . . in the dust, in the cool
   tombs?

Take any streetful of people buying clothes and groceries,
   cheering a hero or throwing confetti and blowing
   tin horns . . . tell me if the lovers are losers . . .
   tell me if any get more than the lovers . . . in the
   dust . . . in the cool tombs.

OLD IRONSIDES

(Written with reference to the proposed breaking up of the famous
U. S. frigate *Constitution*)

Oliver Wendell Holmes

Ay, tear her tattered ensign down!
  Long has it waved on high,
And many an eye has danced to see
  That banner in the sky;
Beneath it rung the battle-shout,
  And burst the cannon's roar:
The meteor of the ocean air
  Shall sweep the clouds no more!

Her deck, once red with heroes' blood,
  Where knelt the vanquished foe,
When winds were hurrying o'er the flood
  And waves were white below,
No more shall feel the victor's tread,
  Or know the conquered knee:
The harpies of the shore shall pluck
  The eagle of the sea!

O better that her shattered hulk
  Should sink beneath the wave!
Her thunders shook the mighty deep,
  And there should be her grave:

Nail to the mast her holy flag,
  Set every threadbare sail,
And give her to the god of storms,
  The lightning and the gale!

THE BATTLE-FIELD

William Cullen Bryant

Once this soft turf, this rivulet's sands,
  Were trampled by a hurrying crowd,
And fiery hearts and armed hands
  Encountered in the battle-cloud.

Ah! never shall the land forget
  How gushed the life-blood of her brave—
Gushed, warm with hope and courage yet,
  Upon the soil they fought to save.

Now all is calm, and fresh, and still;
  Alone the chirp of flitting bird,
And talk of children on the hill,
  And bell of wandering kine, are heard.

No solemn host goes trailing by
  The black-mouthed gun and staggering wain;
Men start not at the battle-cry,
  Oh, be it never heard again!

Soon rested those who fought; but thou
  Who minglest in the harder strife
For truths which men receive not now,
  Thy warfare only ends with life.

A friendless warfare! lingering long
  Through weary day and weary year;

A wild and many-weaponed throng
 Hang on thy front, and flank, and rear.
Yet nerve thy spirit to the proof,
 And blench not at thy chosen lot,
The timid good may stand aloof,
 The sage may frown—yet faint thou not.

Nor heed the shaft too surely cast,
 The foul and hissing bolt of scorn;
For with thy side shall dwell, at last,
 The victory of endurance born.

Truth, crushed to earth, shall rise again;
 Th' eternal years of God are hers;
But Error, wounded, writhes in pain,
 And dies among his worshippers.

Yea, though thou lie upon the dust,
 When they who helped thee flee in fear,
Die full of hope and manly trust,
 Like those who fell in battle here.

Another hand thy sword shall wield,
 Another hand the standard wave,
Till from the trumpet's mouth is pealed
 The blast of triumph o'er thy grave.

THE REVEILLE

Bret Harte

Hark! I hear the tramp of thousands,
  And of armèd men the hum;
Lo! a nation's hosts have gathered
  Round the quick-alarming drum,—
      Saying: "Come,
      Freemen, come!
Ere your heritage be wasted," said the quick-alarming
                                     drum.

"Let me of my heart take counsel:
  War is not of life the sum;
Who shall stay and reap the harvest
  When the autumn days shall come?"
      But the drum
      Echoed: "Come!
Death shall reap the braver harvest," said the solemn-
                               sounding drum.

"But when won the coming battle,
  What of profit springs therefrom?
What if conquest, subjugation,
  Even greater ills become?"
      But the drum
      Answered: "Come!
You must do the sum to prove it," said the Yankee-
                               answering drum.

"What if, 'mid the cannons' thunder,
  Whistling shot and bursting bomb,

When my brothers fall around me,
  Should my heart grow cold and numb?"
        But the drum
        Answered: "Come!
Better there in death united than in life a recreant,
                                    —Come!"

Thus they answered—hoping, fearing,
  Some in faith and doubting some,
Till a trumpet-voice proclaiming,
  Said: "My chosen people, come!"
        Then the drum
        Lo! was dumb;
For the great heart of the nation, throbbing, answered:
                            Lord, we come!"

THE BIVOUAC OF THE DEAD

Theodore O'Hara

The muffled drum's sad roll has beat
  The soldier's last tattoo!
No more on life's parade shall meet
  The brave and fallen few.
On Fame's eternal camping ground
  Their silent tents are spread,
And glory guards with solemn round
  The bivouac of the dead.

No rumor of the foe's advance
  Now swells upon the wind,
Nor troubled thought of midnight haunts,
  Of loved ones left behind;
No vision of the morrow's strife
  The warrior's dreams alarms,
No braying horn or screaming fife
  At dawn to call to arms.

Their shivered swords are red with rust,
  Their plumed heads are bowed,
Their haughty banner, tailed in dust,
  Is now their martial shroud—
And plenteous funeral tears have washed
  The red stains from each brow,
And the proud forms by battle gashed
  Are free from anguish now.

The neighing troop, the flashing blade,
  The bugle's stirring blast,
The charge,—the dreadful cannonade,
  The din and shout, are passed;
Nor war's wild notes, nor glory's peal
  Shall thrill with fierce delight
Those breasts that nevermore shall feel
  The rapture of the fight.

Like the fierce Northern hurricane
  That sweeps the great plateau,
Flushed with the triumph yet to gain,
  Come down the serried foe,
Who heard the thunder of the fray
  Break o'er the field beneath,
Knew the watchword of the day
  Was "Victory or death!"

Rest on, embalmed and sainted dead,
  Dear is the blood you gave—
No impious footstep here shall tread
  The herbage of your grave.
Nor shall your glory be forgot
  While Fame her record keeps,
Or honor points the hallowed spot
  Where valor proudly sleeps.

Yon marble minstrel's voiceless stone
  In deathless song shall tell,
When many a vanquished year hath flown,
  The story how you fell.
Nor wreck nor change, nor winter's blight,
  Nor time's remorseless doom,
Can dim one ray of holy light
  That gilds your glorious tomb.

DO NOT WEEP, MAIDEN, FOR WAR IS KIND

from *War Is Kind*

Stephen Crane

Do not weep, maiden, for war is kind.
Because your lover threw wild hands toward the sky
And the affrighted steed ran on alone,
Do not weep.
War is kind.

    Hoarse, booming drums of the regiment,
    Little souls who thirst for fight—
    These men were born to drill and die.
    The unexplained glory flies above them;
    Great is the battle-god, great—and his kingdom
    A field where a thousand corpses lie.

Do not weep, babe, for war is kind.
Because your father tumbled in the yellow trenches,
Raged at his breast, gulped and died,
Do not weep.
War is kind.

    Swift-blazing flag of the regiment,
    Eagle with crest of red and gold,
    These men were born to drill and die.
    Point for them the virtue of slaughter,
    Make plain to them the excellence of killing,
    And a field where a thousand corpses lie.

Mother whose heart hung humble as a button
On the bright splendid shroud of your son,
Do not weep.
War is kind.

SONG OF THE BRAVE

Laurence Altgood

Sing of the brave and the miracles they wrought;
Sing of the battle nobly fought;
Waste no tear on the coward's grave!
Save your heart for the deathless brave.

THE MARINES' SONG

Author Unknown

From the Halls of Montezuma
To the shores of Tripoli
We fight our country's battles
On the land as on the sea.
First to fight for right and freedom
And to keep our honor clean;
We are proud to claim the title
Of United States Marines.

Our flag's unfurled to every breeze
From dawn to setting sun;
We have fought in every clime and place
Where we could take a gun.
In the snow of far-off Northern lands
And in sunny tropic scenes;
You will find us always on the job—
The United States Marines.

Here's health to you and to our Corps
Which we are proud to serve;
In many a strife we've fought for life
And never lost our nerve.
If the Army and the Navy
Ever look on Heaven's scenes,
They will find the streets are guarded
By United States Marines.

THE CAISSON SONG

Major Edmund L. Gruber

Over hill, over dale, we have hit the dusty trail,
And those caissons go rolling along.
In and out, hear them shout, "Counter march and right
about!"
And those caissons go rolling along.

Chorus:

Then it's hi! hi! hee! in the field artillery,
Sound off your numbers loud and strong.
Where e'er you go you will always know
That those caissons are rolling along.
Keep them rolling! And those caissons go rolling along.
Then it's Battery Halt!

Through the storm, through the night, up to where the
doughboys fight,
All our caissons go rolling along.
At zero we'll be there, answering every call and flare,
While our caissons go rolling along.

Cavalry, boot to boot, we will join in the pursuit,
While the caissons go rolling along.
Action Front, at a trot; volley fire with shell and shot,
While those caissons go rolling along.

But if fate me should call, and in action I should fall,
And those caissons go rolling along.

Fire at will, lay 'em low, never stop for any foe,
While those caissons go rolling along.

But if fate me should call, and in action I should fall,
Keep those caissons a-rolling along.
Then in peace I'll abide when I take my final ride
On a caisson that's rolling along.

THE UNKNOWN SOLDIER

Billy Rose

There's a graveyard near the White House
  Where the Unknown Soldier lies,
And the flowers there are sprinkled
  With the tears from mother's eyes.

I stood there not so long ago
  With roses for the brave,
And suddenly I heard a voice
  Speak from out the grave:

"I am the Unkown Soldier,"
  The spirit voice began,
"And I think I have the right
  To ask some questions man to man.

"Are my buddies taken care of?
  Was their victory so sweet?
Is that big reward you offered
  Selling pencils on the street?

"Did they really win the freedom
  They battled to achieve?
Do you still respect that Croix de Guerre
  Above that empty sleeve?

"Does a gold star in the window
  Now mean anything at all?

I wonder how my old girl feels
  When she hears a bugle call.

"And that baby who sang
  'Hello, Central, give me no man's land'—
Can they replace her daddy
  With a military band?

"I wonder if the profiteers
  Have satisfied their greed?
I wonder if a soldier's mother
  Ever is in need?

"I wonder if the kings, who planned it all
  Are really satisfied?
They played their game of checkers
  And eleven million died.

"I am the Unknown Soldier
  And maybe I died in vain,
But if I were alive and my country called,
  I'd do it all over again."

IN FLANDERS FIELDS

John McCrae

In Flanders fields the poppies blow
Between the crosses, row on row,
   That mark our place; and in the sky
   The larks, still bravely singing, fly
Scarce heard amid the guns below.

We are the Dead. Short days ago
We lived, felt dawn, saw sunset glow,
   Loved and were loved, and now we lie
   In Flanders fields.

Take up our quarrel with the foe:
To you from failing hands we throw
   The torch; be yours to hold it high.
   If ye break faith with us who die
We shall not sleep, though poppies grow
   In Flanders fields.

REPLY TO IN FLANDERS FIELDS

John Mitchell

Oh! sleep in peace where poppies grow;
The torch your falling hands let go
Was caught by us, again held high,
A beacon light in Flanders sky
That dims the stars to those below.
You are our dead, you held the foe,
And ere the poppies cease to blow,
We'll prove our faith in you who lie
  In Flanders Fields.

Oh! rest in peace, we quickly go
To you who bravely died, and know
In other fields was heard the cry,
For freedom's cause, of you who lie,
So still asleep where poppies grow,
In Flanders Fields.

As in rumbling sound, to and fro,
The lightning flashes, sky aglow,
The mighty hosts appear, and high
Above the din of battle cry,
Scarce heard amidst the guns below,
Are fearless hearts who fight the foe,
And guard the place where poppies grow.
Oh! sleep in peace, all you who lie
  In Flanders Fields.

And still the poppies gently blow,
Between the crosses, row on row.
The larks, still bravely soaring high,
Are singing now their lullaby
To you who sleep where poppies grow
In Flanders Fields.

ANOTHER REPLY TO IN FLANDERS FIELDS

J. A. Armstrong

In Flanders Fields the cannons boom,
And fitful flashes light the gloom;
While up above, like eagles, fly
The fierce destroyers of the sky;
With stains the earth wherein you lie
Is redder than the poppy bloom,
    In Flanders Fields.
Sleep on, ye brave! The shrieking shell,
The quaking trench, the startling yell,
The fury of the battle hell
Shall wake you not, for all is well;
Sleep peacefully, for all is well.

Your flaming torch aloft we bear,
With burning heart and oath we swear
To keep the faith, to fight it through,
To crush the foe, or sleep with you,
    In Flanders Fields.

AMERICA'S ANSWER

R. W. Lilliard

Rest ye in peace, ye Flanders dead.
The fight that ye so bravely led
We've taken up. And we will keep
True faith with you who lie asleep
With each a cross to mark his bed,
  In Flanders fields.

Fear not that ye have died for naught.
The torch ye threw to us we caught.
Ten million hands will hold it high,
And Freedom's light shall never die!
We've learned the lesson that ye taught
  In Flanders fields.

THE FIRST DIVISION MARCHES,
September 1919

Grantland Rice

The last to leave—the first to go—
  So is their laurel wrought;
And now they march back home below
  The skies for which they fought;
The skies of home which shed their blue
  Upon the steel-shod clan,
The same blue steel that swept them through
  Cantigny to Sedan.

Not all of them. Somewhere in France,
  Beyond the mist-hung shore,
Stained crosses mark the last advance
  Of those who come no more;
In Soissons drifts, by Argonne streams,
  Or Cheppy's wooded glen,
Beneath his helmet each one dreams
  That he is home again.

The gaps are filled—each in his place
  Will hear the wild acclaim;
With all the valor of their race,
  They played the crimson game;
But when the first gray shadows creep,
  Send one prayer on before,
Where rust-red rifles guard the sleep
  Of those who come no more.

For those who march will turn to find
   Some ghostly mate in vain;
Some buddy who was left behind
   To face the winter rain;
And spring shall bring "blue days and fair"
   Where star-dust crowns their night;
But they shall neither know nor care
   Who hold Valhalla's height.

MEMORIAL DAY

William E. Brooks

I heard a cry in the night from a far-flung host,
From a host that sleeps through the years the last long sleep,
By the Meuse, by the Marne, in the Argonne's shattered
                                                          wood,
In a thousand rose-thronged churchyards through our land.
Sleep! Do they sleep? I know I heard their cry,
Shrilling along the night like a trumpet blast:

"We died," they cried, "for a dream. Have ye forgot?
We dreamed of a world reborn whence wars had fled,
Where swords were broken in pieces and guns were rust,
Where the poor man dwelt in quiet, the rich in peace,
And children played in the streets, joyous and free.
We thought we could sleep content in a task well done;
But the rumble of guns rolls over us, iron upon iron
Sounds from the forge where are fashioned guns anew;

"New fleets spring up in new seas, and under the wave
Stealthy new terrors swarm, with emboweled death.
Fresh cries of hate ring out loud from the demagogue's
                                                          throat,
While greed reaches out afresh to grasp new lands.
Have we died in vain? Is our dream denied?
You men who live on the earth we bought with our woe,
Will ye stand idly by while they shape new wars,
Or will ye rise, who are strong, to fulfill our dream,
To silence the demagogue's voice, to crush the fools

Who play with bloodstained toys that crowd new graves?
We call, we call in the night, will ye hear and heed?"

In the name of our dead will we hear? Will we grant them
sleep?

WRITTEN IN A TIME OF CRISIS

(World War II)

Stephen Vincent Benét

It's a long way out of the past and a long way forward.
It's a tough way, too, and there's plenty of trouble in it.
It's a black storm crowding the sky and a cold wind
                              blowing,
Blowing upon us all.
See it and face it. That's the way it is.
That's the way it'll be for a time and a time.
Even the easy may have little ease.
Even the meek may suffer in their meekness.
But we've ridden out storms before, and we'll ride out this
                              one.
Ride it out and get through.
It won't be done by the greedy and the go-easies.
It'll be done by the river of the people,
The mountain of the people, the great plain
Grown to the wheat of the people.
It'll be done by the proud walker, Democracy,
The walker in proud shoes.
Get on your feet, Americans, and say it!
Forget your grievances, wherever you are,
The little yesterday's hates and the last year's discord.
This is your land, this is your independence,
This is the people's cause, the people's might.
Say it and speak it loud, United, free . . .

ATLANTIC CHARTER: 1942

Francis Brett Young

What were you carrying, Pilgrims, Pilgrims?
What did you carry beyond the sea?
  We carried the Book, we carried the Sword,
  A steadfast heart in the fear of the Lord,
  And a living faith in His plighted word
  That all men should be free.

What were your memories, Pilgrims, Pilgrims?
What of the dreams you bore away?
  We carried the songs our fathers sung
  By the hearths of home when they were young,
  And the comely words of the mother-tongue
  In which they learnt to pray.

What did you find there, Pilgrims, Pilgrims?
What did you find beyond the waves?
  A stubborn land and a barren shore,
  Hunger and want and sickness sore:
  All these we found and gladly bore
  Rather than be slaves.

How did you fare there, Pilgrims, Pilgrims?
What did you build in that stubborn land?
  We felled the forest and tilled the sod
  Of a continent no man had trod
And we established there, in the Grace of God,
The rights whereby we stand.

What are you bringing us, Pilgrims, Pilgrims?
Bringing us back in this bitter day?
  The selfsame things we carried away:
  The Book, the Sword,
  The fear of the Lord,
  And the boons our fathers dearly bought:
  Freedom of Worship, Speech and Thought,
  Freedom from Want, Freedom from Fear,
  The liberties we hold most dear,
  And who shall say us Nay?

JOHN FITZGERALD KENNEDY

John Masefield

All generous hearts lament
    the leader killed,
The young chief with the
    smile, the radiant face,
The winning way that turned
    a wondrous race
Into sublimer pathways,
    leading on.
Grant to us life that though
    the man be gone
The promise of his spirit be
    fulfilled.

THE NEED OF THE HOUR

Edwin Markham

Fling forth the triple-colored flag to dare
The bright, untraveled highways of the air.
Blow the undaunted bugles, blow, and yet
Let not the boast betray us to forget.
Lo, there are high adventures for this hour—
Tourneys to test the sinews of our power.
For we must parry—as the years increase—
The hazards of success, the risks of peace!

What do we need to keep the nation whole,
   To guard the pillars of the State? We need
   The fine audacities of honest deed;
The homely old integrities of soul;
The swift temerities that take the part
Of outcast right—the wisdom of the heart;
Brave hopes that Mammon never can detain,
Nor sully with his gainless clutch for gain.

We need the Cromwell fire to make us feel
   The common burden and the public trust
   To be a thing as sacred and august
As the white vigil where the angels kneel.
We need the faith to go a path untrod,
The power to be alone and vote with God.

THE SHIP OF STATE

from *The Building of the Ship*

Henry Wadsworth Longfellow

Thou, too, sail on, O Ship of State!
Sail on, O UNION, strong and great!
Humanity with all its fears,
With all the hopes of future years,
Is hanging breathless on thy fate!
We know what Master laid thy keel,
What Workmen wrought thy ribs of steel,
Who made each mast, and sail, and rope,
What anvils rang, what hammers beat,
In what a forge and what a heat
Were shaped the anchors of thy hope!
Fear not each sudden sound and shock,
'T is of the wave and not the rock;
'T is but the flapping of the sail,
And not a rent made by the gale!
In spite of rock and tempest's roar,
In spite of false lights on the shore,
Sail on, nor fear to breast the sea!
Our hearts, our hopes, are all with thee,
Our hearts, our hopes, our prayers, our tears,
Our faith triumphant o'er our fears,
Are all with thee,—are all with thee!

AMERICAN MUSE

Stephen Vincent Benét

American muse, whose strong and diverse heart
So many men have tried to understand
But only made it smaller with their art,
Because you are as various as your land,

As mountainous-deep, as flowered with blue rivers,
Thirsty with deserts, buried under snows,
As native as the shape of Navajo quivers,
And native, too, as the sea-voyaged rose.

Swift runner, never captured or subdued,
Seven-branched elk beside the mountain stream,
That half a hundred hunters have pursued
But never matched their bullets with the dream,

Where the great huntsmen failed, I set my sorry
And mortal snare for your immortal quarry.

You are the buffalo-ghost, the broncho-ghost
With dollar-silver in your saddle-horn,
The cowboys riding in from Painted Post,
The Indian arrow in the Indian corn,

And you are the clipped velvet of the lawns
Where Shropshire grows from Massachusetts sods,
The grey Maine rocks—and the war-painted dawns
That break above the Garden of the Gods.

The prairie-schooners crawling toward the ore
And the cheap car, parked by the station-door.

Where the skyscrapers lift their foggy plumes
Of stranded smoke out of a stony mouth,
You are that high stone and its arrogant fumes,
And you are ruined gardens in the South

And bleak New England farms, so winter-white
Even their roofs look lonely, and the deep,
The middle grainland where the wind of night
Is like all blind earth sighing in her sleep.

A friend, an enemy, a sacred hag
With two tied oceans in her medicine-bag.

They tried to fit you with an English song
And clip your speech into the English tale.
But, even from the first, the words went wrong.
The catbird pecked away the nightingale.

The homesick men begot high-cheekboned things
Whose wit was whittled with a different sound,
And Thames and all the rivers of the kings
Ran into Mississippi and were drowned.

They planted England with a stubborn trust,
But the cleft dust was never English dust.

Stepchild of every exile from content
And all the disavouched, hard-bitten pack
Shipped overseas to steal a continent
With neither shirts nor honor to their back,

Pimping grandee and rump-faced regicide,
Apple-cheeked younkers from a windmill-square,

Puritans stubborn as the nails of Pride,
Rakes from Versailles and thieves from County Clare,

The black-robed priests who broke their hearts in vain
To make you God and France or God and Spain.

These were your lovers in your buckskin-youth,
And each one married with a dream so proud
He never knew it could not be the truth
And that he coupled with a girl of cloud.

And now to see you is more difficult yet
Except as an immensity of wheel
Made up of wheels, oiled with inhuman sweat
And glittering with the heat of ladled steel.

All these you are, and each is partly you,
And none is false, and none is wholly true.

AMERICA WAS PROMISES

Archibald MacLeish

America was promises—to whom?

Jefferson knew:
Declared it before God and before history:
Declares it still in the remembering tomb.
The promises were Man's: the land was his—
Man endowed by his Creator:
Earnest in love; perfectible by reason:
Just and perceiving justice: his natural nature
Clear and sweet at the source as springs in trees are.
It was Man the promises contemplated.
The times had chosen Man: no other:
Bloom on his face of every future:
Brother of stars and of all travelers:
Brother of time and of all mysteries:
Brother of grass also; of fruit trees.
It was man who had been promised; who should have.
Man was to ride from the Tidewater; over the Gap:
West and South with the water; taking the book with him:
Taking the wheat seed; corn seed; pip of apple:
Building liberty a farmyard wide;
Breeding for useful labor; for good looks;
For husbandry; humanity; for pride—
Practicing self-respect and common decency. . . .

America was promises to whom?
Old Man Adams knew. He told us—
An aristocracy of compound interest

Hereditary through the common stock!
We'd have one sure before the mare was older.
"The first want of every man was his dinner:
The second his girl." Kings were by the pocket.
Wealth made blood made wealth made blood made wealthy.
Enlightened selfishness gave lasting light.
Winners bred grandsons: losers only bred! . . .

For whom the promises? For whom the river?
"It flows west! Look at the ripple of it!"
The grass "So that it was wonderful to see
And endless without end with wind wonderful!"
The Great Lakes; landless as oceans; their beaches
Coarse sand; clean gravel; pebbles;
Their bluffs smelling of sunflowers: smelling of surf;
Of fresh water; of wild sunflowers . . . wilderness.
For whom the evening mountains on the sky;
The night wind from the west; the moon descending?

Tom Paine knew.
Tom Paine knew the People.
The promises were spoken to the People.
History was voyages toward the People.
Americas were landfalls of the People.
Stars and expectations were the signals of the People. . . .

        Believe

America is promises to
Take!
America is promises to
Us
To take them
Brutally
With love but
Take them.

O believe this!

THE MORAL WARFARE

John Greenleaf Whittier

When Freedom, on her natal day,
Within her war-rocked cradle lay,
An iron race around her stood,
Baptized her infant brow in blood
And, through the storm which round her swept,
Their constant ward and watching kept.

Then, where our quiet herds repose,
The roar of baleful battle rose,
And brethren of a common tongue
To mortal strife as tigers sprung,
And every gift on Freedom's shrine
Was man for beast, and blood for wine!

Our fathers to their graves have gone;
Their strife is past—their triumph won;
But sterner trials wait the race
Which rises in their honored place—
A moral warfare with the crime
And folly of an evil time.

So let it be. In God's own might
We gird us for the coming fight,
And, strong in Him whose cause is ours
In conflict with unholy powers,
We grasp the weapons He has given,—
The Light, and Truth, and Love of Heaven!

GOD, GIVE US MEN!

Josiah Gilbert Holland

God, Give us men! A time like this demands
Strong minds, great hearts, true faith and ready hands;
  Men whom the lust of office does not kill;
Men whom the spoils of office cannot buy;
  Men who possess opinions and a will;
Men who have honor; men who will not lie;
Men who can stand before a demagogue
  And damn his treacherous flatteries without winking!
Tall men, sun-crowned, who live above the fog
  In public duty and in private thinking;
For while the rabble, with their thumb-worn creeds,
Their large professions and their little deeds,
Mingle in selfish strife, lo! Freedom weeps,
Wrong rules the land and waiting Justice sleeps.

UNMANIFEST DESTINY

Richard Hovey

To what new fates, my country, far
  And unforeseen of foe or friend,
Beneath what unexpected star
  Compelled to what unchosen end,

Across the sea that knows no beach,
  The Admiral of Nations guides
Thy blind obedient keels to reach
  The harbor where thy future rides!

The guns that spoke at Lexington
  Knew not that God was planning then
The trumpet word of Jefferson
  To bugle forth the rights of men.

To them that wept and cursed Bull Run,
  What was it but despair and shame?
Who saw behind the cloud and sun?
  Who knew that God was in the flame?

Had not defeat upon defeat,
  Disaster on disaster come,
The slave's emancipated feet
  Had never marched behind the drum.

There is a hand that bends our deeds
  To mightier issues than we planned:

Each son that triumphs, each that bleeds,
  My country, serves Its dark command.

I do not know beneath what sky
  Nor on what seas shall be thy fate:
I only know it shall be high,
  I only know it shall be great.

AUTHOR INDEX

TITLE INDEX

FIRST LINE INDEX